THE GREATEST

MUHAMMAD ALI

THE GREATEST

MUHAMMAD ALI

WALTER DEAN MYERS

SCHOLASTIC
FOCUS

New York

THANKS TO BURT SUGAR, BOXING HISTORIAN, FOR HIS EARLY ENCOURAGEMENT; AND BILLY GILES, MIDDLEWEIGHT, AND JIMMY DUPREE, LIGHT HEAVYWEIGHT, FOR THEIR PATIENCE AND INSIGHTS.

First Scholastic paperback printing, November 2001

ISBN 978-1-338-29014-1

5 4 3   22 23 24

Printed in the USA   37

This edition first printing 2018

Book design by Kristina Albertson

TO RUDINE SIMS BISHOP IN APPRECIATION
OF HER YEARS OF FRIENDSHIP.

—W.D.M.

CONTENTS

INTRODUCTION

Heroes that looked anything like me were hard to come by when I was a kid growing up in Harlem. I remember Sugar Ray Robinson, then the welterweight champion, stopping his flashy Cadillac on our block and sparring with me and the other kids. All the kids on the block loved his playing with us, even the girls. Once in a while I would spot heavyweight champ Joe Louis on 125th Street near the Apollo Theater in New York City and that was always a thrill. But Robinson and Louis were relatively simple men, their brilliance limited to their exploits in the ring. Another Robinson, Jackie, had just integrated major league baseball and became, for me, the most exciting male figure in the African-American community until the Summer Olympics of 1960.

That summer, a young man would stand on the podium, a gold medal around his neck, while the "Star

Spangled Banner" played. A caption on the television screen I watched announced that Cassius Clay had won the gold medal in boxing. It was the first glimpse for most Americans of the man who would come to be known as The Greatest.

In examining the life of Muhammad Ali, there are many vantage points from which to study this remarkable man. Race, politics, religion, and the fight game itself are the arenas in which Ali's mark was indelible in my mind and, I believe, in the national consciousness as well. Ali's private life — his three failed marriages, his relationships with children, especially his own — has often been placed under public scrutiny. In his private life, Ali is revealed to be a man of human faults and human weaknesses. I appreciate the "normal" Muhammad Ali, but I choose to write about The Greatest.

And it was as The Greatest that Ali has had the greatest impact on our culture and on the sport of professional boxing. A humbler man would have pleased the sports-writers more. A man who would not mention race would have made many Americans more comfortable.

"As a young black, at times I was ashamed of my color, I was ashamed of my hair," the baseball great Reggie Jackson once said, "and Ali made me proud."

At a time when the civil rights movement was noted for its turn-the-other-cheek, nonviolent stance, young black men saw in Ali the possibility of reclaiming their manhood. For young Americans with growing doubts about the war in Vietnam, he expressed their misgivings.

But Ali was a fighter, the heavyweight champion, in a sport which destroyed its heroes. Joe Louis was severely brain-damaged when he died in 1981. Ray Robinson, my Ray Robinson who had played with us on the streets, suffered from Alzheimer's disease when he died in 1989. Jerry Quarry, who fought against Ali, is said to have died in a "punch-drunk fog" in 1999. When I contacted Floyd Patterson's office to gather material for this book, I learned that he, too, suffered from brain damage. I spoke briefly with Joe Frazier at a party in Philadelphia and wondered about his gently slurred speech. This was the game that Ali mastered, and to which he gave so much of himself.

Today, Muhammad Ali suffers from Parkinson's disease. Was boxing, the scene of his most magnificent triumphs, also the genesis of his toughest challenge? While no one can be sure, I wonder and I worry for Ali and for all of the young men still to enter the fight business. It is the cruelest of sports.

In writing this book, I have decided to look at the public Muhammad Ali, the man who represented so many views, who personified the needs of so many Americans but, most of all, the Muhammad Ali who most touched me. I look upon him as an American, as a fighter, as a seeker of justice, as someone willing to stand up against the odds, no matter how daunting those odds, no matter how big his foe. In writing this book, I realized that, over the years, I have admired and yes, even loved Muhammad Ali. I still do.

Walter Dean Myers

Jersey City, New Jersey
May 2000

FLOAT LIKE A BUTTERFLY . . .

Cassius Marcellus Clay *acted like a madman at the weigh-in. He was screaming at the top of his lungs, his eyes rolled wildly, the veins bulged in his neck. The doctor measuring his heart rate noted that it was twice what it usually was: His blood pressure had climbed to 200. It was February 25, 1964, the morning of The Fight in Miami Beach.*

"He's terrified!" a sportswriter announced.

There was talk that the fight shouldn't be allowed to go on. Cassius Clay would be too terrified, the old-timers said, to be effective. Sonny Liston would kill him. Clay's handlers tried to calm him as he lunged around the room.

"Float like a butterfly, sting like a bee!" Clay shouted into the face of his buddy Drew "Bundini" Brown. Angelo Dundee, Clay's white trainer, stood to the side, watching with amazement.

"Float like a butterfly, sting like a bee!" they yelled at each

other at close range as busy photographers recorded the strange goings-on. "Rumble, young man, rumble!"

Sonny Liston, the thirty-one-year-old champion, looked across the room at Clay and shook his head. His mind went back to the previous July just before his fight in Las Vegas. He had been losing money in the casino, and the young fighter Clay had taunted him from the sideline. Liston had walked over to Clay, stood face-to-face with him, and told him that if he didn't get away from him in ten seconds, he was going to rip his tongue out of his mouth and shove it somewhere. Clay shut up instantly and quickly moved away.

"I think you got his attention," a friend of Liston's said.

"I got more than that," Liston growled. "I got the punk's heart."

And it sure seemed that way at the weigh-in. Clay, who had just reached his twenty-second birthday, seemed close to collapsing from nervousness. Photographers shot dozens of pictures, and sportswriters were busily taking notes. The young man from Louisville, Kentucky, was a seven-to-one underdog, and some were wondering if he would even show up later for the fight.

Sonny Liston was the world heavyweight champion and one of the most feared fighters in America. He had faced Floyd Patterson for the championship in 1962 and had knocked him out in the first round. He had faced Patterson a second time in 1963 and again had knocked him out in the first round.

A fearsome puncher, Liston had been an enforcer for organized crime, or the Mob, before turning pro, making sure that

Mob-protected businesses had no labor trouble. If you wanted someone hurt, if you wanted someone intimidated, you sent for Sonny Liston. He had served time for armed robbery and had been arrested for fighting a cop, for assault, and for drunkenness. He had long, heavily muscled arms and could knock a man out with a jab. He had destroyed good fighters on his way to the championship, and now he was going to face a twenty-two-year-old who had never fought a major heavyweight.

At fight time, the betting odds overwhelmingly favored Liston. As they entered the ring, the physical differences between the two men were immediately obvious. Liston was a hulk of a man with huge arms and legs and a face that sent shivers up the spine. He had the face of a thug. He glowered at Clay. It was the same look he had used when he collected debts for the Mob. It was the stare that made seasoned fighters look away.

Clay, on the other hand, was handsome, almost pretty. At six feet three, he was two inches taller than Liston, and at 210 pounds, he was eight pounds lighter. His breathing seemed shallow as he listened to the referee's pre-fight instructions.

The referee told the two men to shake hands and come out fighting.

Clay came out of his corner and instantly started moving from side to side. Liston, his biceps and shoulders glistening with sweat, came after him. Clay threw a quick jab into Liston's face, and Liston threw a hard right. It hit nothing but air as Clay danced lightly away.

Liston's jab was a heavy, punishing blow, and he threw it once, twice. Each time it was short of the mark. Clay jabbed again, connected, and followed it with two quick blows to the heavyweight champion's face.

Liston swung furiously, missing again. The ring was small, but Liston knew he had to make it even smaller. As Clay moved to the champ's left, Liston tried to cut him off. Too slow. Clay hit him — once, twice, three times — and then moved away. At the end of the round, Clay went back to his corner and sat down heavily. He was breathing hard. Was he tired? Nervous? The crowd didn't yet know what to make of the young challenger.

Round two. Clay was moving again, bouncing from side to side, moving just out of the reach of Liston's punches. He was embarrassing the champ. Liston started a jab and then stopped it. He started a right hand, realized that he wasn't going to hit Clay with it, and stopped it in midair. Clay threw two quick jabs and a hard right.

At ringside the spectators were wondering what they were seeing. Clay looked like a master boxer, and Liston the champion looked slow and plodding. Could Clay actually dance away from Liston for the whole fight?

Suddenly, Liston caught Clay on the ropes. Clay pulled Liston's head toward him and down. Liston was inches from the "punk" he had wanted to shut up. He threw a flurry of savage punches into Clay's body. Clay got off the ropes, and Liston rushed after him. Again, the lightning jabs from Clay, punching down at Liston. A quick right hand stopped Liston in his tracks, and suddenly he was backing up from Clay.

Liston tried to dance, to show that he could move. But his movements were nothing compared with Clay's, who had promised he would "Float like a butterfly, sting like a bee!"

By the end of the second round the spectators in Miami Beach were stunned. Liston was cut under his left eye! He looked tired. But he hadn't really tagged Clay yet. Just wait, they thought. Sooner or later Liston would catch up with the brash young fighter and knock him out.

The start of the third round had Clay again dancing around his slower opponent. Clay would lean back, allowing Liston's punches to miss by less than an inch, then counterpunch sharply. Liston was lunging. He tried to push Clay into a corner. Clay, surprisingly strong, again grabbed Liston and pushed his head down. Clay took Liston's body punches until he could move away. But the body punches didn't seem to do much harm.

Round four. The two fighters were in close, and suddenly Clay was blinking furiously. He was backpedaling, rubbing his eyes. What was wrong? He stopped jabbing and looked close to panic. Liston threw one heavy punch after another.

At the end of the round, Clay's eyes were closed.

"Cut them off! Cut them off!" Clay said, referring to the gloves. "I can't see! I can't see!"

Angelo Dundee, Clay's trainer, looked at his fighter's eyes. They were red and tearing. Dundee thought perhaps some astringent from Liston's face had gotten into Clay's eyes and tried to wash them out. Clay kept blinking.

"I can't see!" Clay said again.

"They'll clear up," Dundee said.

"I can't fight if I can't see!" Clay protested.

"If you can't fight, run," Dundee shouted.

The rest time was up, and Dundee pulled Clay to his feet for the fifth round. The young fighter went to the middle of the ring, still blinking furiously, trying to find Liston through the tears. Liston came across the ring like a mad bull, putting everything he had in every punch. Clay pushed him away, leaned back, and let Liston hit him in the body. Liston threw overhand rights and left hooks that just missed Clay's chin.

The crowd was going wild. It was clear that Clay was in trouble. But still, Liston couldn't finish him off. The round ended, and Clay stumbled back to his corner. His cornermen worked feverishly on his eyes, trying to wash out whatever it was that was blinding Clay.

Dundee was frantic, trying to get his fighter back into the ring.

"This is the big one," he pleaded, knowing that if Clay quit, the young fighter might never get another chance for the title. "You're fighting for the championship!"

By the middle of the sixth round, the stinging in Clay's eyes had subsided. So far he had survived half-blind in the ring with the man who had crushed some of the best heavyweights in the country. As Clay's vision cleared, his confidence grew. Everything he had learned in his brief ring career, from the neighborhood gym in Louisville to his training as a pro, all came together. Suddenly it was Clay who was the master, the toreador, and Liston the clumsy buffoon.

The sixth round found Liston puffing heavily. Few of his fights had ever gone that far — he usually knocked his opponent out within three rounds. Clay moved expertly around the ring, arms down by his sides, leaning just out of the way of Liston's punches. Liston's face was puffy and bleeding where Clay's stinging punches found their mark.

At the end of the sixth round Dundee was reassuring his fighter, telling him just to continue to do what he was doing: Keep on floating like a butterfly, keep on stinging like a bee.

Clay looked across the ring at Liston, who was slumped on his stool. Then, suddenly, Clay stood up and raised both arms over his head. He started skipping around the ring. He had seen Sonny Liston spitting out his mouth protector.

The fight world was stunned. Liston, the champ, had quit. Cassius Marcellus Clay was now the world heavyweight champion.

What had happened? Some people said that there had been a fix.

In Clay's dressing room there was pandemonium. Reporters were trying to get in, calling out their questions. An exuberant Clay was screaming to the world that he was the king.

In Liston's dressing room his handlers tried to stop the bleeding from the cut on his face. The cut was real. So was the sweat and the blood and the pain. This was not what Liston, or anyone else, for that matter, had expected.

"Who is this guy?" he wondered aloud.

Part I

CASSIUS CLAY

Every living being was born to accomplish a certain purpose, and it is the knowing of the purpose that enables every soul to fulfill it.

— Casslus Clay

A BOXER'S DREAM

The heavy black headlines of the Louisville *Courier-Journal* were filled with war news. Pearl Harbor had been attacked the month before, and the United States, which had been at peace since 1919, now found itself at war with both Japan and Germany. Young men across the country were volunteering to join the army, and the young men of Louisville, Kentucky, were no exception.

Louisville, for most Americans, was known for the Kentucky Derby, the annual thoroughbred horse race. Race day at Churchill Downs, the stadium in which the derby was run, was a day of celebration and parties. The race itself was always preceded by the singing of the state song, "My Old Kentucky Home."

> *The sun shines bright in my old Kentucky home*
> *'Tis summer, the darkies are gay. . . .*

But on Saturday evening, January 17, 1942, Cassius Clay's mind was not on the war or the Derby. His wife, Odessa, affectionately called "Bird," had just given birth to a baby boy in Louisville City Hospital. Cassius decided to give the boy his own name. He would be called Cassius Marcellus Clay, Jr.

The name Clay was a famous one in Kentucky. Henry Clay had twice run for president and had served in Congress for over twenty-five years. Cassius Marcellus Clay, although the son of a slaveholder, had been part of the antislavery movement. He published an abolitionist newspaper, the *Examiner,* in Louisville. He was also one of the founders of the Republican Party in 1854.

Cassius Clay, Sr., named after the abolitionist, worked as a sign painter in Louisville. He prided himself on his work and had painted murals in many of the local black churches. His wife, Odessa, had been doing mostly domestic work since her teen years and attended a local Baptist church. The Clays lived on Grand Avenue, a quiet street in the west end of the city. While not in the professional class, the Clays were doing moderately well when the new baby arrived. But how well a black family could do was limited by segregation.

Under segregation, black people were not allowed to eat in "white-only" restaurants, or attend the same schools, or even sit with whites on public transportation or in movie theaters. This separation of people by race was legal and was enforced by the law. This did not mean that whites and blacks did not get along. People, white and black, understood the "rules" of segregation, and both races knew where they were welcome and where they were not. Cassius Clay, Sr., understood that he might never have a real relationship with a white person. He might work for a white man, or have a conversation with one, but the relationship would stop at the end of the day, or at the end of the line, or at whatever breaking off point maintained the status quo between whites and blacks. It was under this system of "knowing one's place" that Cassius Jr., and his younger brother, Rudolph, would grow up. It would influence both of them greatly.

Cassius was a shy child. His early school days were not particularly eventful. He was not, like some fighters, a childhood bully, but a good kid with a sensitivity to injustice.

In 1954, twelve-year-old Cassius rode his red-and-white Schwinn bicycle to the Columbia Auditorium in Louisville. He and a friend visited The Louisville Home Show, which was a predominately black trade show. There was free candy and popcorn, and a general air of excitement as local merchants displayed their goods. When it was time to go, Cassius found that his bicycle was missing.

The Schwinn company made the most popular bicycles in the country, and Clay was angry and hurt that his had been stolen. The chance of his family scraping together the money for a new bicycle was slight, and Cassius was so upset that he was crying.

He wanted to report the bicycle stolen and was told

that there was a policeman in the basement. Cassius found the officer, Joe Martin, and told him what had happened. He also added that when he found whoever had stolen his bike, he was going to beat him up.

Joe Martin had been a member of the Louisville police force for years. He enjoyed working with young people, black and white, and taught boxing at the Columbia Gym.

"You thinking about beating somebody up, you had better learn to fight," he told the eighty-nine-pound Cassius. That suited the boy. He wanted to teach the bike thief a lesson and in his twelve-year-old mind he could imagine himself beating up the perpetrator. Cassius started boxing lessons.

Men who spend their lives teaching boys are a special breed. There is often a tenderness about them that is never expressed but that the child can understand. Joe Martin was such a man. At first, he didn't think much of the new boy's skills. Cassius was skinny and awkward. A lot of the other boys beat him in the ring; some beat him easily. But there was one thing that was different. Cassius would show up at the gym like clockwork — none of the other boys were as dedicated. Whatever work Martin asked of him he did, and then some. Soon, he was training six days a week with Martin and also with a black man named Fred Stoner.

One of the most difficult things for mature black men to see is the downward spiral of young black boys. Some react by turning away, by denying that it is happening. Others just angrily blame the kids. Still others, remembering the sweet language of youth, reach out and offer a helping hand to the hearts expecting disappointment and to the minds that have learned not to trust. Fred Stoner, at the Grace Community Center in Louisville, was one of the black men reaching out to young boys in the fifties and sixties.

One of the problems for black boys was that there were so few outlets for them. Too many children had nothing to do after school, and trouble waited in the streets. The Grace Community Center gave them a place to be, to hang out, to be safe. It also gave young Cassius Clay a place to learn more about boxing.

Cassius found out about the Grace Center and was eager to see what he could learn from it. He and his brother, Rudolph, began to go to both gyms: the Columbia Gym with Joe Martin, where Cassius would train as hard as he could, and then the Grace Center.

What Fred Stoner learned about Cassius — which Martin already knew — was that the loud-mouthed kid who liked to brag about what he would do to an opponent was absolutely dedicated to boxing. He practiced for long hours, perfecting each move he was taught, learning how to control himself physically in the ring.

Where Joe Martin, the patrolman, was a tough guy and expected his young fighters to be tough, Fred Stoner was more schooled in the ways of boxing. He knew that Cassius Clay's dream depended on more than his determination, even when he saw him training as much as six days a week. Cassius spent a lot of time with Stoner and appreciated what the black man was offering him.

Stoner liked Cassius and his brother. He guessed that the Clay boys, who didn't drink or smoke, came from the same economic background as the other boys who hung around the center. Young black boys, such as Cassius and Rudolph, who had working-class parents, didn't go to symphonies and ballets. They grew up with little exposure to outside cultural influences.

"I suppose Clay was a hungry fighter," Stoner said. "He didn't come out of an affluent family. He didn't have it too easy. We're all out of the same bag."

What Stoner perhaps suspected, and what the world was yet to know, was that boxing would bring young Cassius Clay out of the cultural ghetto. Boxing would change his life forever.

Joe Martin remembered that nothing seemed to discourage Cassius. Once, he was knocked unconscious but returned the next day to train against the boy who had knocked him out.

Martin produced a local television show, *Tomorrow's Champions,* and young Cassius began to appear on it. He won some fights and lost others. Two years later Cassius's dedication to training and his determination to improve were still there, but he wasn't yet anything special.

To boost his own confidence he bragged a lot. He told other young fighters that they couldn't beat him, that they couldn't hurt him. He wasn't a particularly hard puncher, but that didn't stop him from announcing that he was going to knock out anyone he faced.

By the time Cassius turned sixteen, things had changed. He was still thin, he was still a light hitter, but he had reflexes and a coordination that old professionals in the field had never seen. He still lost fights, but even the officials who ruled against him saw that he was good.

Cassius was devoting more and more of his time to boxing. The winner of two national AAU (Amateur Athletic Union) titles, six Kentucky Golden Gloves, and two Golden Gloves championships, his mind was set on a boxing career. He dropped out of high school in March 1958. Central High's tenth grade was not as attractive as the upcoming Olympics. He was being noticed by fight fans around the country.

By his eighteenth birthday, in 1960, there was no doubt about Cassius Clay's boxing skills. There were still problems with his technique, though. Instead of moving away from punches the way most fighters did, he would simply lean back, judging the distance and velocity the punch would travel as it came toward his chin. It was a fundamental mistake. If, in the heat of battle, he judged wrong, he could have been hit hard. But he was fast enough to get out of harm's way: His reflexes were as sharp as anyone had ever seen.

It takes more than boxing skills to be a fighter. It takes the courage to stand up to an opponent, knowing that he wants to use his talent to hurt you as badly as he can. It also takes the ability to deal with two aspects of pain: the anticipation that you will be hurt, perhaps badly, and the knowledge that you can stop more pain simply by quitting. Cassius seemed to have the skills and the courage, and that's what it would take to qualify for the Olympics, which were to be held that summer in Rome.

To get to the Olympics he had to go through a series of fights, meeting the best amateur fighters from around the country. Only one fighter from each weight group would be sent to represent the United States. The finals of the trials were to be held in California. But Joe Martin, still working with Clay, discovered a problem: Cassius was afraid of flying. Martin convinced Cassius that there - wasn't time for a long train ride across the country. During the turbulent flight, Martin had to work hard to calm the young man down. It worked. Clay won the trials and qualified to go to Rome.

Clay wasn't heavy enough in 1960 to enter the Olympics as a heavyweight. Instead, he was entered in the 178-pound light heavyweight division. He won his first three fights fairly easily. Clay had trained hard for the

Training for the 1960 Olympic Games.

Olympics. Even in the Olympic village he stayed up late at night to shadowbox in his room while his boxing teammates slept. His style — straight, crisp punches and avoiding being hit — impressed the international judges. But the fourth fight proved difficult.

Olympic matches only have three rounds. A fighter is scored by how many times he hits his opponent cleanly and by his ability to avoid being hit. The fighter who wins two rounds almost always wins the match because it is extremely difficult to knock out an opponent in three rounds.

The Polish challenger, Zbigniew Pietrzykowski, was a European champion and had won a bronze medal four years earlier in the 1956 Olympics. Pietrzykowski was tough and plowed into the inexperienced Clay. The left-handed Polish fighter's strength and mauling style made Clay look bad. He clearly lost the first round.

Clay tried the same quick jab-and-move tactics in the second round and realized that he was receiving as much punishment as he was giving. He had dreamed of the glory of being a champion, and this was his chance. He didn't want to lose.

He made a small change in style, setting his feet more firmly in order to throw harder punches. He had to stop the Pole's oncoming rush. At the end of the second round it wasn't clear who was ahead.

Clay came out in the third and final round with the determination that was to become his trademark. He used every bit of the skill and nerve he had to take control of the fight. The end of round three left Pietrzykowski battered and helpless against the ropes.

The 1960 games in Rome were a turning point in Olympic coverage with the emergence of two black stars. One was the tall sprinter from Tennessee State University, Wilma Rudolph. An outstanding athlete, Rudolph was a hit with Americans across the country as she won gold medals in three events. The other star was Cassius Clay.

At the medal ceremony, eighteen-year-old Cassius Clay looked like a child next to the older men he had beaten. The fight had been broadcast on television all over the world. People who knew next to nothing about the sport now knew about a young man from Louisville named Cassius Clay.

The Olympic team flew back home from Rome to New York. When Clay returned to the United States, his world had turned completely around.

What was happening to him? The young man from the segregated South who was used to being banned from certain restaurants and parks because he was black, was now being celebrated. In New York he visited Harlem for the first time and met Sugar Ray Robinson, considered by many to be the greatest fighter, pound for pound, who had ever entered a ring.

Sugar Ray Robinson was handsome and flashy. He liked to drive his lavender-colored Cadillac convertible slowly through the streets of Harlem, stopping now and again to spar with young boys, shaking hands, and generally accepting the enthusiastic appreciation of his fans. Before the Olympics and the gold medal, Clay had glimpsed the kind of attention a famous boxer could receive. When he returned he was getting much of the same attention.

At eighteen, the world seemed his for the taking.

Back home, a group calling itself the Louisville Sponsoring Group agreed to back Clay in his professional career. The group consisted of eleven men. They were white and southerners, but they were also people who were willing to look out for a young black man from their home state.

Clay received a $10,000 signing bonus from the group and was guaranteed a $333-per-month draw against his future earnings. In addition, 15 percent of his income would be put into a pension plan for him.

At the time, for boxing, and for professional sports of any kind, this was a great deal for Clay. Most beginning fighters were lucky to clear $200 a fight at the start of their careers, and none of them got a signing bonus. Very often they would have to take menial jobs that would interfere with their training. Clay, through the help of the Louisville Sponsoring Group, could concentrate solely on boxing.

THE HARD FIGHT

There are two sides of boxing. On one side are the winners, trying to hold on to the money they make, trying to maintain their health. On the other side are the losers, with both money and health slipping away. Archie Moore, the man selected by the Louisville Sponsoring Group to be Cassius Clay's new trainer, knew both sides of the game.

Archie Moore was born in Benoit, Mississippi, on December 13, 1913. He was raised by his aunt and uncle in St. Louis, Missouri, and began boxing in reform school. His professional boxing career began in 1936. Life was hard for all Americans during the depression years that began in 1929 and didn't end until World War II. Boxing was a way of making a few dollars during those years, but it was nothing like the lucrative sport it would become. The young Moore worked a number of jobs as a laborer, sometimes taking fights with just a day's notice.

Boxing has a number of economic levels. There are the "headline" fights of the major box office draws. These are the fights of which the international sports community takes note and which command high "purses," or payments for fights, for the fighters. There is usually a major effort to promote these events to the general public, and the fighters are often well known. All fighters want to reach this level because of the money to be made. Fighters and managers at the top are never eager to fight someone from a lower level. The mid-level fights feature lesser-known boxers, and there is often pressure for the reigning champions in each weight division to fight the top contenders. At the bottom of the game are the fighters who scramble for matches and who fight for a few dollars while holding down full-time jobs.

The goal for the young fighter is to get a bout with an upper-level opponent. Archie Moore found himself in the ring with the same fighters over and over again because the top fighters would simply ignore him. But for Archie and for most young fighters, boxing had two irresistible lures. The first was the hope for a big payday and the match that would propel the man who often scrubbed floors to eat, into the big time — the good life of fancy clothes, a pocket full of money, and celebrity. The downside of this dream is that few fighters make money at boxing. A typical mid-level purse in the 1960s might have been a mere $2,500. From this the boxer had to pay his training expenses, cornermen, medical expenses, equipment, travel expenses, and give perhaps as much as 40 to 50 percent to his manager. He was lucky if he broke even. At the lowest levels even to this day, fighting is for little more than a few extra dollars of spending money.

The second lure of boxing was the same for the fighter as for the fan — the sport itself, the exciting, primitive appeal of two men fighting in a ring. Civilized men might control their impulses to hit people, deny the rush that violence can sometimes produce. But in the ring it was, and still is, allowed. The best fighters are invariably those who can most easily break down the barriers of control we have all been taught, who can bring a rage to the ring, a willingness to smash a man into unconsciousness, to see him fallen and bleeding on the canvas. To fight on a professional level you have to want to hurt people. You have to want to see the helpless look in a fighter's eyes as you send yet another punch in his direction. Professional boxing is a sport of blood and pain and more pain. It is a sport in which naked brutality is the norm. If a fighter doesn't love it, he needs to be in a different place.

The dark side of this issue is obvious. While it is the boxer's desire to batter his opponent without mercy, it is also his opponent's aim to do the same. The cost to the human body is staggering. As Archie Moore observed, "Your body just has a certain number of hard fights in it."

In amateur boxing the fighters are required to wear protective headgear. Points are scored by the landing of blows, and not by the force behind the blows or the effect. A knockdown is not considered more significant than any other blow, and knockouts are rare. In professional boxing the *force* of the blows, especially to the head, are more highly regarded by the judges than lighter blows. Knockouts, especially in the heavyweight class, are the name of the game. A knockout, simply put, is an injury to the brain that renders the sufferer incapable of standing up. Sometimes a fighter can sustain an injury to the brain sufficient to make him unaware of what is going on while still able to stand, and therefore vulnerable to even more punishment. Referees are constantly looking at fighters' eyes to see if they are "out on their feet."

Archie Moore was forty-seven when Cassius Clay arrived at his camp in November 1960, sent by the Louisville Sponsoring Group for training. But Clay had already tasted the kind of fame he had longed for, had seen the lights of Harlem and those of the press corps. He had seen his image in *Sports Illustrated* and on television and was growing to love it. Now he was at the spartan camp of Moore, who had been fighting longer than Clay had been alive, and who wanted to teach the young star defensive fighting.

Clay trained in the Salt Mine, Moore's aptly named camp in Ramona, California. Moore tried to teach Clay his way of avoiding punches. But every fighter comes to his own style based upon his own visions of himself and assessment of his skills. Moore saw himself as a survivor, and indeed he was, having survived an amazing twenty-four years in the ring. He stayed low in the ring, using his arms and shoulders to absorb punches as he moved into his opponent — taking the punches to his arms and body did not put him at risk of being knocked out or sustaining career-ending injuries. He had seen too many boxers who were "punch-drunk" after even a few years of fighting, and knew what an accumulation of blows to the head could do to a man.

Clay didn't think that Archie Moore was wrong in what he was teaching. But what the young fighter understood, better than anyone else, was the range of his own skills and how those skills made him feel confident in the ring.

Sugar Ray Robinson was considered one of the best fighters who had ever lived. He had the uncanny ability to punch with devastating force while moving backward. His hand speed and combinations were legendary. He was an attractive, flashy fighter, and Clay was impressed by the middleweight's popularity.

Clay's style, the style he was developing, also had a strong defensive element. He had fantastic hand speed and foot speed. His physical coordination, his ability to move around the ring, was impressive for a man his size. "Float like a butterfly, sting like a bee!" was more than a clever slogan; it was a technique that would take him to the very top of the boxing world. But Archie Moore worried that Clay's fabulous speed would one day fade, or be slowed by fatigue in the closing rounds of a long fight. Still, speed was Clay's game. It fit his personality. He didn't want to stand toe-to-toe and slug it out with an opponent. He wanted to frustrate the men he fought, to mess with their minds as they swung at him and missed. Clay was also confident that he could figure out the styles of the men he would fight and undermine their strengths. While he understood there would be bigger, stronger fighters than he was, he felt that the combination of his physical skills and his understanding of the fight game would defeat any opponent.

When Cassius Clay went home from Moore's camp for the Christmas holiday, he knew he would never return.

"THE GREATEST"

As impressive as the young Clay's Olympic experience was, there were two events that had occurred, years before, in May 1954, that perhaps had the most influence on him. In Southeast Asia, the fall of Dien Bien Phu, in Vietnam, signaled the French defeat and the beginning of American involvement in a long and bitter war. The United States at first sent soldiers to Asia as "advisers" to the South Vietnamese army. As the war escalated, however, it became clear that Americans would also have to serve as combat soldiers. Many people felt that the United States should not have been involved in that war and did not want to support it either financially or by entering the armed forces.

At home the issue of race loomed large. The Supreme Court's ruling to end school segregation with the *Brown vs. the Board of Education* decision should have meant new opportunities for African Americans. The truth of the matter, though, was that southern schools refused to allow African Americans to register, and that new lawsuits were being filed to force integration. The civil rights movement was growing within the United States as the Vietnam War was intensifying in Asia. Both events would affect Clay deeply.

In 1962, Cassius Clay looked younger than his twenty years. His appearance, handsome to the point of being "pretty," as he called himself, was a marked contrast to his chosen profession. The youthful Clay, joking with his fans, reciting his poetry on television, looked to all the world like a friendly kid — not a menacing fighter. His good looks and his playfulness helped Clay attract a following far different from fighters who preceded him. Young people, black and white, especially identified with the brash young man from Louisville. Many of his new fans had never followed boxing before. The idea of two men beating each other senseless was not a sport for - everyone, but Clay made it different.

The media, especially, took to Cassius Clay. Unlike the usual array of heavyweight fighters who spoke poor English or in monosyllabic grunts, Clay ran his mouth a mile a minute.

"I am The Greatest!" he would shout at anyone who would listen.

The press didn't always appreciate Clay's shouts and rants. Some sportswriters were open in their disgust for

Clay. Who was this bragging fool? They couldn't wait until someone shut up the Louisville Lip.

Love him or hate him, the press was writing about Clay, and he understood the importance of publicity. He was becoming a media sensation. Writers began to wonder who the real Cassius Clay was. Was he an insignificant clown just looking for a big payday in boxing? When Clay claimed that he was The Greatest, was he referring to the greatest fighter or the greatest human being?

By 1962, Clay had not proven himself as a boxer against a major opponent. There were fight professionals who thought he had superior skills, but skills alone did not make anyone The Greatest. What would happen when he faced an opponent at the top of the game, whose skills were as good as his and who would provide the gut check that all fighters eventually face? If they spend enough time in the ring, all fighters reach that moment when they get badly hurt. What would Clay do when his moment came?

Boxing fans and writers always compare fighters, and young Clay was no exception. The chief comparison was with the man who held the heavyweight championship the longest, Joe Louis. Louis's heavyweight career began in 1934, and he won the heavyweight championship in June of 1937. Born Joseph Louis Barrow, Louis, "The Brown Bomber," was a proud, disciplined champion who never bragged about his conquests. His managers advised him never even to smile after a win, especially against a white opponent. During World War II, Louis enlisted in the army and fought ninety-six exhibitions to entertain the troops while raising thousands of dollars in U.S. bonds to support the war effort. America saw Louis as a relatively simple person, one who did not challenge the traditional position of the black man.

Louis's most famous fights were with Max Schmeling, the German heavyweight. On June 19, 1936, the Nazi war machine was gearing up for world domination. Much of the Nazi philosophy dealt with the idea of racial superiority, and the Nazi leader, Adolf Hitler, saw Schmeling as personifying his theme of the master race. When Schmeling knocked out Joe Louis in the twelfth round of their fight, the Nazis were elated.

By 1938, World War II was already raging in Europe, and it seemed likely that the United States would soon be involved. The Nazis were eager to have Schmeling defeat Louis again and become the world champion. The night of the fight, June 22, 1938, millions of black Americans were huddled around their radios hoping for "their Joe" to defeat the German. They didn't have to wait long. Louis knocked out Schmeling in the first round. All of America was proud and relieved that an American had won.

As a fighter Joe Louis was capable of knocking an opponent out with one punch, an ability that Clay had not shown. But it was Joe's dignity that people talked about when they compared the two fighters. Would Clay ever display such dignity?

Another fighter on the scene in 1962 was Charles "Sonny" Liston. Liston was considered by many in boxing insiders as being unbeatable. A massive man with good boxing skills and a crushing punch, he was seen as the most formidable heavyweight fighter. Because of Liston's ties to organized crime, the National Association for the Advancement of Colored People, or NAACP, asked Floyd Patterson, the heavyweight champion at the time, not to fight Liston. Patterson, a man dedicated to the sport of boxing, felt that all contenders deserved a chance at the crown.

For Cassius Clay, the 1960s had begun with the Olympics, a gold medal, and international fame. By the beginning of 1962 he had already won ten professional fights against carefully selected opponents. Another Olympic gold medalist, Floyd Patterson, had lost the heavyweight championship to the powerful Swede Ingemar Johansson and had won it back convincingly with a crushing knockout. Patterson was scheduled to fight Sonny Liston in September 1962, and no one gave the former Olympian much of a chance against the much bigger, hard-hitting Liston.

The September 25 fight between 214-pound Sonny Liston and 189-pound Floyd Patterson ended quickly, with Liston knocking out Patterson in the first round.

Two months later Clay fought his former teacher, the aging Archie Moore.

"I had to fight him for financial reasons," Moore said. "It wasn't what either of us wanted, but I was in a bind financially."

Clay predicted he would knock out the forty-eight-year-old Moore in the fourth round and accomplished that feat. Moore was clearly over the hill, but he still had a measure of respect. People were still wondering just how good Clay really was.

Professional fights are entertainment events, designed to make money. Tickets, television and radio rights, and even film rights are all for sale. Sonny Liston had demolished Floyd Patterson for the championship, and a rematch was scheduled for July 1963. But another Liston-Patterson fight, projected as another early loss for Patterson, was not a big money fight. So the question was, who would be a sufficient challenge to Liston and command the large money a major heavyweight fight could bring? Cassius Clay decided to promote himself as that boxer.

Meanwhile, more and more of the burden of the war in Vietnam fell on American soldiers. The cold war also became more intense as Russian missiles were discovered in Cuba, causing an international crisis. Colonel John H. Glenn became the first American astronaut to go into orbit. In the South, Freedom Riders, civil rights workers attempting to integrate interstate bus lines and train

terminals, were viciously beaten by racists. Police dogs were used to attack African Americans protesting attempts to keep them from voting.

Black athletes, for the most part, were not part of the civil rights movement. Joe Louis did not speak out on racism. Sugar Ray Robinson, like Joe Louis, had served the United States in the army and had fought exhibitions in the States and in Europe during World War II.

Floyd Patterson made a point of being nonpolitical and moved his family to a predominately white neighborhood. He considered himself first and foremost a boxer, and he just wanted to get along with all people. In 1962, however, America was changing. Television was bringing both the civil rights and antiwar movements into American homes. This was the milieu in which twenty-year-old Cassius Clay came to manhood.

Direct involvement in the civil rights movement was not that easy for young African Americans to accomplish. In order to maintain a favorable position with liberal observers, movement leaders such as Dr. Martin Luther King, Jr., James Farmer, and A. Philip Randolph recruited college graduates and other highly educated people. The only major organization that was giving a voice to the "common man" was the Black Muslim group known as the Nation of Islam. In 1962, Clay drove to Detroit and heard the Nation of Islam's leader, the Honorable Elijah Muhammad for the first time. He also met a man who would greatly influence his life, a man called Malcolm X.

Cassius was maturing into manhood. Like all young Americans he saw the racial conflicts throughout the country. He saw more and more young men of his own age question the country's involvement in the Vietnam War. Many older Americans did not know what to make of this younger generation. Nor did they know what to make of a young man running around saying that he was The Greatest.

THE PRICE OF FAME

The year 1963 was a most dramatic one in American history. For Cassius Clay it was a year of important decisions. A week after his twenty-first birthday he fought Charles Powell in Pittsburgh, knocking out the fairly ordinary fighter in the third round. The fight was seen as such an easy bout for Clay that two months later he was in the ring again, this time in New York against Doug Jones, considered by many to be an excellent boxer, but one who lacked the big punch needed to become a champion. Clay predicted that he would knock out Jones in the fourth round: "I'm changing the pick I made before. Instead of six, Doug goes in four!"

The fourth round came, and Clay tried his best to knock out Jones, but failed. In the sixth round, he worked as hard as he could to end it, but it wasn't to be, and the large crowd at Madison Square Garden was clearly disappointed. Clay won the match on points, but some sports fans saw the mediocre fight as a sign of Clay's true ability. He was advised not to predict the round of his next fight, which would take place in London, England, against British heavyweight Henry Cooper. Clay ignored the advice and said that Cooper would fall in the fifth round.

The crowds that Clay had been attracting in the United States were phenomenal. He was giving boxing a much needed shot in the arm as thousands of fans showed up to see this trash-talking young man. The Jones bout had filled Madison Square Garden to capacity. But Clay's reception in England was exceptional, as the twenty-one-year-old boxer was treated like royalty. Cheering crowds stopped traffic as Clay toured the posh downtown sections of London. He realized that he was a celebrity even thousands of miles from home and in another country. He clowned around for a series of publicity photos with the Beatles, the most popular rock 'n' roll group in the world at the time, posed with English dignitaries, and gave endless interviews.

This reception by English fans gave Clay a different idea of his stature. He was being accepted in a much wider population than other sports figures. He was not only young and handsome, but his youth and charm were accessible. He was, in fact, a world figure at twenty-one.

Tuesday, June 18, 1963. The fight with Henry Cooper would reveal much about the young Clay, some of it troubling to those around him. The press had played up the fight, and British crowds were eager to see the real Clay. The beginning of the fight was typical Clay — he was so much faster than Cooper that the fight seemed to be a mismatch. Time and again he had Cooper in trouble, only to back off and go into a kind of dance routine. Some of the producers didn't like Clay's clowning around, thinking it would cheapen the match. But then, at the end of the fourth round, Cooper lunged forward with a tremendous left hook that got Clay hard on the jaw. He fell back into the ropes, dazed. Then, hands lowered, he lurched forward onto the canvas. The crowd was stunned.

Clay was down and confused. He got up, but it was obvious that his head still wasn't completely clear. The bell rang, ending the round, and Clay's handlers helped him back to his corner. He seemed to be in trouble as he slumped onto the stool.

Angelo Dundee, his trainer, put smelling salts under Clay's nose, trying desperately to bring him around. The cornermen put ice on his back and into his trunks, trying to shock him back to full consciousness. Dundee, an expert handler of fighters, thought that Clay might not be able to continue.

Clay's glove had been split earlier, and now Dundee, standing hunched over Clay, opened the split. Then he called it to the referee's attention. "I don't know how much time that got us," Dundee later said. "Maybe a minute, but it was enough."

A minute. A minute for the boxer to recuperate, for the brain to recover from the damage it had been dealt. A boxer is considered knocked out if he is down for a count of ten. Ten long seconds of brain damage so severe that a man cannot perform the simple act of standing up.

The bell rang, finally, for the next round. The split was finally taped, but the delay had given Clay ample time to recover. He came to the middle of the ring and, like a man possessed, threw more punches at Cooper than the English boxer had ever seen before. Cooper was demolished. Mercifully, the referee stopped the fight. Clay raised his fists above his head in victory.

Clay was a star. He was loved by people who knew nothing about the fight game. As the biggest draw in boxing, he was also where the money was. Sonny Liston's - people contacted Clay. A fight for the heavyweight championship of the world was arranged.

Who was Cassius Clay? He was a black man who had grown up in a racist South, who had seen black men reaching for brooms when they should have been reaching for the stars. He was a black man who had felt the humiliation of seeing water fountains from which he could not drink because of the color of his skin.

On August 28, 1963, Clay saw the March on Washington, a national outpouring of support for the civil rights

Next page: The Greatest, 1964.

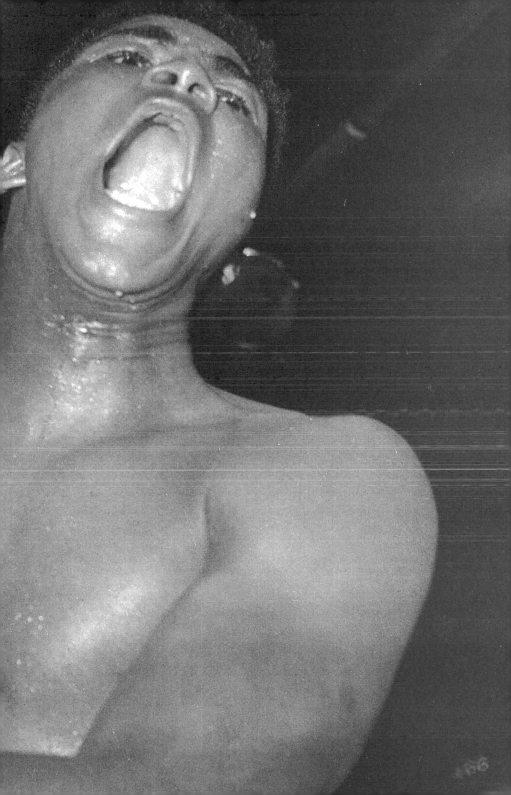

movement. He also saw, less than a month later, the bombing of a black church in Birmingham, Alabama, in which four little girls were killed.

But as Clay observed America in 1963, America was also observing him. Charming, handsome, and a world-class athlete, he was attracting a lot of attention from young people. After the Cooper fight in England, however, he began to see more criticism. Barry Stainback, a writer for *Sport* magazine, asked, "How has Clay come so far and learned so incredibly little about his craft? Simply because he hasn't had to learn anything. [Doug] Jones is the only real fighter Clay's met so far, and he too should've been a setup because of his great lack of height, weight, and reach in comparison to Cassius . . . Some of us would like to buy a large insurance policy on Cassius Clay before he steps in with good old Charley Liston. That could be worth a fortune."

While the sports media questioned Clay's ability, Clay showed his audience a new militant position. In August, at the March on Washington, the Nation of Islam's Malcolm X denounced the nonviolent direction of the civil rights movement. By September it was Clay who spoke against nonviolence: "I'm a fighter. I believe in the eye-for-an-eye business. I'm no cheek turner. I got no respect for a man who won't hit back. You kill my dog, you better hide your cat."

The Nation of Islam was becoming more visible to both Clay and the American public. In 1959, newscaster Mike Wallace, along with Louis Lomax, had produced a program about the Nation of Islam called "The Hate That Hate Produced." This documentary presented to Americans their first open look at the Nation of Islam with its strongly antiwhite sentiments. The theme of the program was that American racism, directed against African Americans, had created a reaction of hatred against whites. The organization most connected with that hate was, said Wallace, the Nation of Islam.

The widely seen television program acknowledged that the leader of the Nation of Islam was the Honorable Elijah Muhammad, but the most outspoken and effective member was the man known as Malcolm X. Malcolm and the Nation of Islam were interested in Cassius Clay because Clay had already taken a political stance in his private life and had shown interest in many of the principles of the Nation of Islam.

By 1963, Clay had been listening to Malcolm X and to ministers from the Nation of Islam for some time. They offered him an alternative both to Christianity and to the position of black people in the United States. While the civil rights movement sought to integrate all Americans, the Nation of Islam favored the separation of the races. Moreover, the Muslims claimed that the black man had sufficient resources in his own community to have a separate nation without becoming part of the white community.

Cassius, not yet twenty-two, understood fully that he was a celebrity and therefore was being sought by the

Muslims at least partially because of his celebrity status. But why was the white community seeking him out? He knew that he made money for people involved in the boxing business. He knew that the offers he was receiving from television stations, from newspapers, from magazines were for the purpose of exploiting his fame. Clay was a fighter, a person used to standing toe-to-toe with an adversary and using his skills to gain a victory.

Perhaps in another year — in 1960 or 1962 — Cassius Clay would have remained Cassius Clay. Perhaps if the black Christian churches had taken a more militant stance, had asked Clay to stand up for Christianity and fought more aggressively against racism, Clay would have taken up the challenge and continued in the religion of his mother. But in 1963 there was a convergence of events, which Malcolm X described as a turning point in the history of black Americans.

A grassroots movement had begun in the black community early in 1963. There was a call for a nationwide protest against injustice in which all black Americans would demonstrate their solidarity. The protest would take the shape of a march on Washington.

As the movement began to gather force, President John F. Kennedy became concerned that a mass gathering of African Americans in the nation's capital would undermine the sympathy shown to the civil rights movement.

Hurried meetings were called and support for the protest was announced. But along with the support came a change in leadership. From the grassroots demonstration, a gathering of ordinary people against racism and injustice, the march became a highly organized assembly of whites and blacks. Malcolm X protested. He said that the march was losing its anger and had become, instead, a carefully controlled gathering of people more interested in loving their enemies than in a revolution.

In June of 1963, Medgar Evers, a black man leading the fight for voting rights for African Americans in Mississippi, was killed in front of his home.

The March on Washington, D.C., held on August 28, 1963, was described by *The New York Times* as having a "picnic quality." Militant black voices, such as the author James Baldwin, were not allowed to speak at the demonstration. The Nation of Islam described the march as a failure. But from that gathering, the country first heard the famous "I Have a Dream" speech of Dr. Martin Luther King, Jr.

On November 22, 1963, President Kennedy, who had supported the black drive for civil rights, was assassinated.

During this chaotic period, America somehow expected Cassius Clay to be nonpolitical. He was an athlete, a boxer, an amusing man-child who should go on entertaining the public with his antics. It was not to be.

Part II

MUHAMMAD ALI

When I left the house of bondage I left everything behind. I wasn't going to keep nothing of Egypt on me, and so I went to the Lord and asked him to give me a new name.

Sojourner Truth

THE CHAMPIONSHIP

Angelo Dundee, Cassius Clay's trainer, noticed the new people Clay was attracting to his camp. They were neatly dressed black men, with close shaven heads, who were always polite but firm. Clay had attended several meetings of the Nation of Islam and had spoken personally with Elijah Muhammad, who ran the organization from his Chicago offices. Sportswriters who questioned Clay on the civil rights movement noted that he was against integration.

"I believe it's human nature to be with your own kind," Clay announced in an interview with *Inside Boxing*.

Sportswriters who liked Clay the brash clown, did not view his militant leanings favorably, and began to write negative things about him. Barry Stainback, of *Sport* magazine, said that the fighters he had beaten were all "setups," men selected as easy wins for Clay. This was in the summer of 1963, right after the March on Washington and after Clay had beaten Henry Cooper in London.

While more and more sportswriters were beginning to distance themselves from Clay because of his political views, they all recognized that he had become an attraction in the heavyweight division. Sonny Liston's handlers knew this as well, and arrangements were made for Clay to fight Liston. The fight was to be held in February 1964, in Miami Beach, Florida.

Mainstream sportswriters wanted Cassius Clay to remain safely tucked away in a niche they found comfortable. They wanted to write about the fight game, about how much money each boxer received for a fight, about knockout punches. They didn't like Clay's bragging, his naming the round in which he would finish an opponent. They wanted someone reasonably quiet who would, from time to time, say something worth printing.

What they got was Muhammad Ali.

As the fight neared, Miami Beach became a publicity circus with reporters from around the world eager to cover the event. Liston — big, mean, and talented — was the overwhelming favorite, but Clay was popular and attractive. He was signed for the fight precisely because of his popularity and for the new audience he was attracting. There would be little money in a fight between the unpopular Liston and an unknown.

On paper it was an easy match for Liston. The thirty-one-year-old fighter had lost only once in the ten years he

Next page: Ali, posed for reporters with his trainers, Angelo Dundee (l.) and Drew Brown, before the fight for the championship against Sonny Liston in Miami Beach, 1964.

43

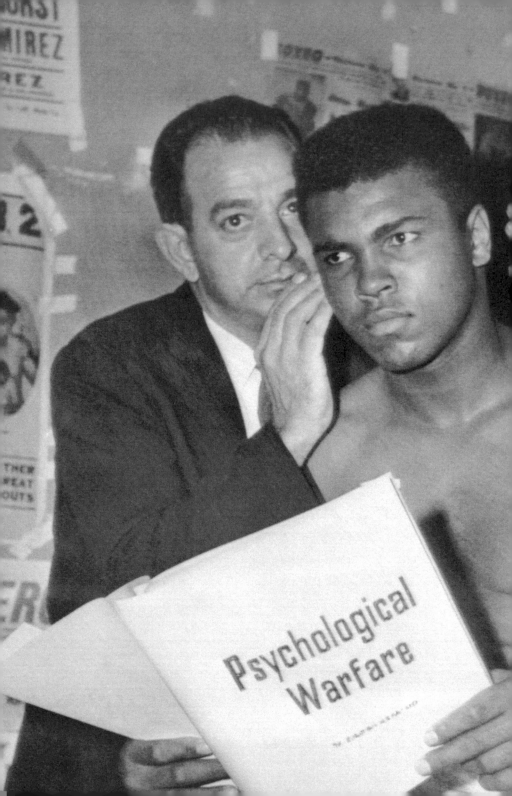

Psychological
Warfare

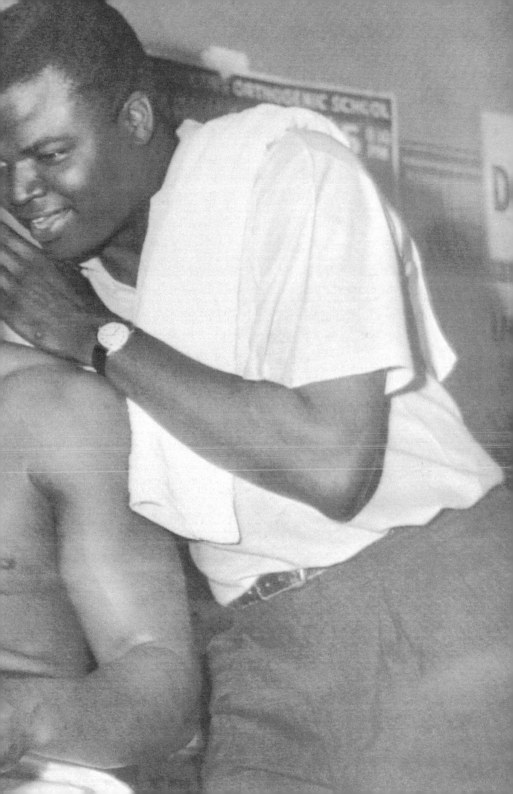

had been fighting professionally. He had knocked out twenty-five of his opponents and had utterly destroyed Floyd Patterson, the previous champion. Liston was a huge man with enormous strength in his massive arms. His style was based on intimidation. His deadly stare was well known and had defeated many of his opponents even before the fights had begun. Cassius Clay, nearly ten years younger than Liston, was affected by the intimidating tactics but somehow managed to bring his own style into play. Before the fight he taunted Liston, calling him "the bear," and verbally defused the famous stare as being "just plain ugly." Liston had much more professional fight experience, but Clay turned this around by saying that Sonny was too old to win.

Clay attracted a lot of young black people who were becoming disillusioned with the civil rights movement. Dr. Martin Luther King, Jr.'s, philosophy of nonviolence for blacks seemed futile against people bent on committing violent acts against black churches and black children. Also, African Americans often took Clay's actions as an expression of race pride. His references to himself as "beautiful" inspired young African Americans and became the impetus of the "Black is Beautiful" movement.

"If he stands and fights, I'll kill him. If he runs, I'll catch him and kill him," Liston answered when asked how the fight would go.

It was in the ring where the two fighters' opposing styles were most obvious. Clay's speed, not Liston's strength, dominated the fight. Liston had good foot speed, but Clay was faster. When, in the fourth and fifth rounds, Clay had been temporarily blinded, Liston caught him on the ropes but still couldn't hurt the younger man. It was a frustrating experience for Liston. When Clay regained his vision in the sixth and began to punish Liston, the fight was over. An exhausted and humiliated Liston failed to come out for the seventh round.

There was pandemonium in the Miami Beach arena after the fight. Reporters rushed to the phones to record the stunning upset. Clay was screaming that he was The Greatest, and everyone was trying to figure out what had happened.

Liston claimed that he had hurt his left shoulder during the fight and couldn't defend himself. Some people were calling for an investigation of the substance that had blinded Clay. (It was probably the astringent used to stop the bleeding from Liston's face that accidentally found its way onto Liston's gloves and into Clay's eyes.) Some sportswriters, still not believing the loudmouthed youth - could beat Liston, wondered if the Mob had influenced Liston to quit. The truth of the matter was that they had just seen a talented fighter, Cassius Clay, rise to the occasion and become a *great* fighter.

It was after the fight in Miami Beach that Clay, now world champion, announced that he had become a Muslim and changed his name to Muhammad Ali.

Changing one's name in sports was common. William

Harrison Dempsey changed his name to Jack Dempsey. Arnold Raymond Cream changed his name to Jersey Joe Walcott. Walker Smith, Jr., became Sugar Ray Robinson. Guiglermo Papaleo became Willie Pep. Joseph Louis Barrow changed his name to Joe Louis. Thomas Rocco Barbella became Rocky Graziano.

Although the sports media had accepted these name changes without hesitation, they refused to accept Muhammad Ali. For years after he changed his name, sportswriters continued to refer to Ali as Clay. They made a point of showing their disapproval of Ali for changing his name for religious reasons and for joining the Nation of Islam.

Ali understood what was going to happen to him when he announced that he was becoming a Muslim and changing his name. He guessed that if he had made the announcement prior to the Liston fight, the match would never have been made. He also knew that he would lose much of the popularity he had enjoyed as a nominal Christian. He had been faced with a clear choice. He could have kept his given name and continued his religious conversion in private, out of the public eye, and enjoyed years of uninterrupted fame. He chose instead to offer up the fame he achieved for what he believed in. It took a great deal of courage, but it was courage that Ali would show time and time again.

Ali's conversion was not taken as a sign that he changed his mind about his religious beliefs. It was felt by many whites and blacks that he had been duped into becoming a Muslim by the Nation of Islam and that the organization would use Ali as a symbol of racial hatred.

The racial undertones that have always been present in America have often affected the fight game. The black boxer Jack Johnson began fighting professionally in 1897 at age nineteen, when white fighters would not fight blacks. He fought for years without having any hope of getting a championship fight. Then, when Tommy Burns was champion, Johnson followed him from country to country, taunting and demanding a match. Finally, a promoter made the match in Sydney, Australia. Johnson beat Burns easily and became the first black heavyweight champion. A search was made for a white person to beat Johnson. James J. Jeffries, who had retired from boxing, was asked to return to the ring as "the Great White Hope" and return the championship to white America.

On July 4, 1910, an out-of-shape Jeffries returned only to lose the match against Johnson. Eventually Johnson was arrested on a trumped-up morals charge and had to leave the country. When he returned he was put into jail for eight months in Kansas. Many believed that his only crime was embarrassing white America.

But if Ali had embarrassed some Americans by joining an organization that preached racial separation, he was still very popular with young people, black and white.

Young men identified with the handsome, charismatic youth in much the same way they did with Malcolm X. Malcolm was that strong voice so long missing among young men in the black community. While Jack Johnson, in his day, had been popular, he had also shown little interest in the conditions of his fellow African Americans. Ali, on the other hand, began his work as a Muslim minister, speaking at various mosques throughout the country and taking a special interest in the welfare of black children. And there was always that marvelous gift for using the media to make himself visible to the world, a vitally important concept to people who so often felt invisible.

A rematch with Liston was scheduled. Somehow, in his defeat, Liston, the bad guy, the brute, was now the good guy. The fight was scheduled for November 16, 1964, but three days before the fight Ali had severe pains in his stomach. He began to vomit and asked to be taken to the hospital. When he arrived, the doctors examined him and found an inguinal hernia. There was a tear in the muscles lining his stomach, and the intestines had broken through. The pain was intense, and Ali was rushed into surgery.

"If he'd stopped all that hollering, he wouldn't have a hernia," Liston said. The fight was rescheduled for May 25, 1965.

Meanwhile, the Nation of Islam was in turmoil. Malcolm X had broken with the organization in 1964 and had been feuding with its leader, Elijah Muhammad.

Then, on a cold February day in 1965, Malcolm X was assassinated in New York City. There was talk within the black community of a coming battle between various factions of the Muslim movement. Would Ali be caught up in the hate and violence? The promoters of the rematch with Liston had sought a large market, but state after state turned the fight down because of Ali's ties to the Nation of Islam. The fight was finally scheduled to take place at a small youth center in Lewiston, Maine.

Security was tight as fight time approached. People still had doubts about Ali's skills and Liston was the betting favorite. Many people were hoping that Ali would lose because of who he was, rather than what his skills were.

President Lyndon B. Johnson had signed the Civil Rights Act into law on July 2, 1964. The law offered more opportunities for blacks to enter the mainstream of American life, which most African Americans wanted, while the Nation of Islam was suggesting that African Americans build their own communities and businesses. But most African Americans were Christian, as was Dr. Martin Luther King, Jr., the most important leader in the civil rights movement. There were, in older black Christian Americans, mixed feelings about the young Muslim Ali.

Fight night. Ali was in terrific shape. While Liston looked despondent and dour, Ali, with his thirty-four-inch waistline and powerful arms, seemed to have taken on the role of intimidator.

The fight started with Ali using the same tactics that had clinched the championship for him in Miami Beach. He moved, he jabbed, he moved more. Liston jabbed, threw some hard punches that didn't land on the elusive target, and tried to maneuver Ali into the ropes. Suddenly Ali stepped to the right and threw a quick, downward punch. Liston went down.

"Get up and fight, sucker!" Ali yelled as he stood over the fallen Liston.

Liston didn't get up. Jersey Joe Walcott, the ex-fighter who was refereeing the match, tried to push Ali away to a neutral corner. Finally, Ali moved away and Liston struggled to his feet. Seventeen seconds had passed. Ten seconds is all a fighter is allowed. The fight was over.

"The punch jarred him," Ali said afterward. "It was a good punch, but I don't think I hit him so hard he - couldn't have gotten up."

Muhammad Ali had come to the fight in the best shape of his life. He was twenty-three years old, at the height of his physical powers. He had fought twenty professional fights and close to one hundred amateur fights. He had a style that he could impose on Liston, and the physical and mental skills to do it. Liston had been intimidated not by Ali's physical presence, but by the prospect of facing a situation in which he could not win.

Ali would have one more fight in 1965: In November

The rematch: Heavyweight champ Ali knocked Sonny Liston out in one minute in the first round.

he would go up against Floyd Patterson, the former world heavyweight champion.

In an October 1965 article in *Sports Illustrated,* Patterson commented, "I have nothing but contempt for the Black Muslims and that for which they stand. The image of a Black Muslim as the world heavyweight champion disgraces the sport and the nation. Cassius Clay must be beaten and the Black Muslims' scourge removed from boxing."

Patterson's remarks hurt and angered Ali. He saw himself as being for the black man one-hundred percent and - didn't like having his racial integrity questioned. Ali claimed that he had no racial animosity against anyone, no matter their race or religion. His trainer, Angelo Dundee, was white. Ali had white friends among the sportswriters. But that wasn't good enough for Patterson, who asserted that he would regain the championship for Christianity.

Ali took his revenge on November 22, 1965. He pounded Patterson without mercy, backing off each time Patterson looked like he could be knocked out. Finally, the referee ended the fight in the twelfth round. Ali had won in a technical knockout. It was not a popular victory — a lot of sportswriters wanted to see Patterson win. Moreover, they wanted to see Ali return to being Cassius Clay. But what they saw was the best fighter in the world.

"WHAT'S MY NAME?"

The 1960s were a turbulent decade, the decade in which the public learned to say no to the government's war in Vietnam and to injustice in America, and yes to peace, love, and rock 'n' roll. What's more, most of the real action centered around young people. Young people called "flower" children in the streets of San Francisco rocked to the raucous sounds of Janis Joplin in the Fillmore West, and marched the streets in protest against the Vietnam War. Americans who had reached their eighteenth birthday had to register for the draft and were issued draft cards. Antiwar protestors burned their draft cards to show their disapproval of the war in Vietnam. Black people wore huge Afros, and hippies wore flowers. In the South, African-American children marched in the streets along with their elders, and college students sat at the lunch counters waiting to break the barriers of segregation.

For most Americans each action was not only a statement in itself, but also a symbol. Some of the symbols became so popular that they were instantly recognized. For some people, a brightly colored Volkswagen "Bug" decorated with peace signs and flowers brought smiles of recognition: Here was a peace-loving, groovy person in an in-your-face car who was probably into hip music and love between all people.

But the peace movement had its detractors. To those Americans not used to questioning what their government did, protesting the war was close to treason. To others, the idea that blacks were no longer willing to accept second-class citizenship was a symbol of social decline.

One of the major symbols of the sixties was the name changes among members of the Nation of Islam. Malcolm X had been born Malcolm Little, in Omaha, Nebraska. The name Malcolm had been given to him by his parents, but the name Little was, Malcolm said, a hand-me-down from the days of slavery. Most members of the Nation of Islam took the X, which stood for their unknown African names. When Cassius Clay became a Muslim, he also took a new name, Muhammad Ali. The symbolism of the name change suggested a more militant turn to the civil rights movement.

Arenas that had begged for fights now turned down matches that involved Ali. In March 1966, Ali went to Toronto, Canada, to fight against George Chuvalo. Two months later he had a second fight with Henry Cooper in

London. Ali won the match on a technical knockout when Cooper was so badly cut and bleeding that he could not continue the fight.

On August 6, 1966, Ali defeated Brian London, another British heavyweight. The match lasted only three punishing rounds. A month later, on September 10, he beat Karl Mildenberger, in Frankfurt, Germany. In England, in all of Europe, Ali's popularity was growing. His name change did not have the same symbolism abroad as it did in the United States. His personality was seen in Europe as just an extension of American brashness.

Meanwhile, back home, there was increased resistance to the civil rights movement. Protest marchers were being hit by police billy clubs and tear gas. In June 1966, a civil rights worker, James H. Meredith, was shot as he led marchers on a pilgrimage from Memphis, Tennessee, to Jackson, Mississippi. In October 1966, the Black Panther party was formed in Oakland, California. Declaring themselves to be for the "self defense" of black people, the Panthers openly carried rifles, demonstrating a major escalation of militancy among young blacks in the civil rights struggle.

Ali was finally allowed to fight in Houston, Texas, in November. Cleveland Williams had been a world-class fighter and a great puncher, but had had numerous problems outside of the ring. In 1964, before his fight with Ali, he had been severely injured by gunshots in a street disturbance. He recovered in time for the fight but was knocked out by Ali in three rounds.

Early 1967. The news from Vietnam was not good. Young Americans were being killed at an alarming rate in a war that it seemed we could not win. The news from the civil rights frontlines looked just as bleak. For every victory there was a setback. More and more blacks were arming themselves, fearful of a race war. To many Americans, the young fighter from Louisville, Kentucky, represented all that was bad about the era. Ali was openly against the war and he gave a face and a voice to the country's racial problems. The problem for many Americans was not that blacks were forced into second-class citizenship but that they made themselves visible by protesting that deprivation of rights.

On February 6, 1967, Ali fought against Ernie Terrell, who had made a point of telling the press that he would not call the man he knew as Cassius Clay by any other name. Terrell, a rangy heavyweight, had little chance against Ali. But his taunts were damaging Ali's reputation. Sportswriters were publishing "interviews" with fighters who really expressed their own dismay over Ali's joining the Nation of Islam.

"What's my name? What's my name?" Ali put the question to Terrell over and over again as he beat him mercilessly in front of the same sportswriters who had encouraged Terrell to make his statements about Ali.

Sportswriters such as the well-known Jimmy Cannon took the occasion to say that Ali was racist and mean-spirited. And, safe from Ali's fists, he had the courage to call him Cassius Clay. He made no mention of Terrell's remarks about Ali. Ali was not acting the way sportswriters thought he should, and they were going to punish him for it in the press.

Cassius Clay had registered for the draft on April 18, 1960, as required by law. He was given a 1-A classification on March 9, 1962. This is the classification everyone is given until they undergo physical and mental tests to see if they are fit for military service. On January 24, 1964, he was ordered to the Armed Forces Induction Center in Coral Gables, Florida, where he took a qualifying examination. Clay scored below the qualifying scores on the standardized aptitude tests at that time and again in March 1964.

In February 1966, Clay (as he was still known to the draft board) was reclassified 1-A, the draft board now saying that his test scores were acceptable. Ali appealed the classification and also asked for status as a conscientious objector, or "CO" status. Conscientious objectors were those who, due to their religious or moral beliefs, could not participate in military service. This request was denied, and Ali asked for a hearing. A hearing was held on

August 23, 1966. Ali had to convince the hearing officer that three things were true: The first was that he was sincere in his objection to military service; the second was that his objection was based on religious training and belief; and the third was that his religious beliefs were against all wars.

In a written statement and then in answer to questions put to him by the hearing officer, Ali said he understood that by refusing to enter the army he was seriously injuring his reputation and ability to earn a living. He went on to say that as a Muslim he objected to participation, in any way, in any war.

The Koran, the holy text of the Muslim religion, forbids the taking of a life, and the participation in any war that is not in defense of the Muslim faith. Ali put this forth to the hearing officer. And, to the surprise of many, the hearing officer recommended that Ali be given CO status. Despite the recommendation, his appeal was turned down by the draft board.

Throughout the country, other young men were protesting U.S. participation in the Vietnam War. Some were fleeing to Canada; others went underground to avoid a war they felt was morally wrong. Thousands of draftees applied for and received CO status based upon their religious beliefs. But Muhammad Ali had become a symbol of the antiwar movement. He was also a superstar. Young men and women who did not like his allegiance to the Nation of Islam still respected his decision to make what they saw was a positive racial statement in changing his name. In the late sixties, especially in the inner cities, few young blacks had involvements with whites. They might not subscribe to the racial theories of the Nation of Islam, but neither were they very much affected by those theories. The draft board feared that if Ali was given CO status then all the members of the Nation of Islam could claim such a status.

The date for Ali's induction into the army was set for April 28, 1967. In an interview for the April 10 edition of *Sports Illustrated*, Ali was asked how he felt about the Vietnam War. "Why should they ask me to put on a uniform and go ten thousand miles from home and drop bombs and bullets on brown people in Vietnam while so-called Negro people in Louisville are treated like dogs?" he asked.

An army induction ceremony is a simple affair. All of the inductees stand in lines and a military officer calls out their names. When an inductee's name is called, he steps forward. When everyone in the group has made the symbolic step forward, there is a swearing-in ceremony. If an inductee does not step forward, he is said to have refused induction and is then charged with a federal crime.

The draft board listed Ali's name as Cassius Marcellus Clay, and that was the name called. Muhammad Ali refused to step forward.

"Freedom means being able to follow your religion, but

Next page: Ali at the Army Induction Center in Houston.

U.S. POST OFFICE →

U.S. CUSTOMS ←

MEETING THE
Challenge
of the
LATER YEARS

senior citizens month

MAY 1967

NEW INTERNATIONAL POSTAGE RATES

EFFEC... 1967

NEW R... E L... ...AVAILAB...
...T... ...OW

DOES NOT...

PO...Form...

NOTICE

YOUR ADDED CONVENIENCE --- YOUR NEW

HR. SELF SERVICE POST OFFICES

ARE LOCATED AT

...ERLAND SHOPPING CENTER
SOUTH POST OAK AND BEECHNUT
AND

...EY'S ALMEDA/GENOA CENTER
GULF FREEWAY AT ALMEDA/GENOA ROAD

Granville W. Elder...
POSTMASTER

it also means carrying the responsibility to choose between right and wrong," he said. "So when the time came for me to make up my mind about going in the army, I knew - people were dying in Vietnam for nothing and I should live by what I thought was right. I wanted America to be America."

Because Joe Louis fought exhibitions and helped raise money for the government during World War II, and because Sugar Ray Robinson had been assigned to what the army called Special Services, Ali was privately assured that he would be used only to raise the morale of troops. He would play the same role during the Vietnam War as Joe Louis and Sugar Ray Robinson had played during World War II. His stance would have been seen as heroic to many.

A group of elite black athletes, including football great Jim Brown and basketball stars Bill Russell and Lew Alcindor (who would later become a Muslim and take the name Kareem Abdul-Jabbar), called a meeting to talk to Ali. Some of them advised the young boxer to go into the army. It would be better than jail, they reasoned, and he would maintain his status as heavyweight champion. The feeling of many of the athletes prior to meeting with Ali was that he was a youth being taken advantage of by the Nation of Islam. However, after the meeting, they left with the realization that he was indeed young, but firm in his convictions and willing to live with the consequences of his actions.

Ali, as he said he would, did not step forward when asked to by the officials of the draft board. After a two-day trial in June 1967, in which he was found guilty of refusing induction, he was given the maximum sentence of five years' imprisonment and a fine of $10,000. He was released pending an appeal of the case, and his passport was taken away.

His heavyweight championship was taken away by the World Boxing Association. Muhammad Ali, unbeaten in the ring, had finally fallen.

A FIGHTER'S EXILE

Within weeks of Muhammad Ali's conviction and the removal of his championship status, each state revoked his boxing license. Sportswriters, athletes, politicians, and entertainers joined in condemning Ali. He was called a coward, a traitor, and a racist. His lawyers appealed the case, but if he lost the appeal Ali would have to serve the five years in jail. His character was suddenly considered not good enough for professional boxing.

But fighters who had been convicted of armed robbery were considered of good enough character to enter the ring. Fighters who had been convicted of murder made a living fighting.

Besides his stance on the draft, Ali's attachment to the Nation of Islam continued to be problematic to many middle-class African Americans. Those who had expressed a liking for Cassius Clay, now tried to create a distance between themselves and Muhammad Ali.

Many African Americans also did not want to risk alienating President Lyndon B. Johnson by opposing the war in Vietnam. Others saw the war as draining resources that could be used for the war on poverty, a much more pressing issue to the black community than the conflict in Southeast Asia.

Ali began to lecture within the Nation of Islam and at colleges throughout the nation. He spoke about social issues, the war in Vietnam, and on the hate that he was accused of spreading.

"I don't hate nobody and I ain't lynched nobody," he stated. "We Muslims don't hate the white man. It's like we don't hate a tiger; but we know that a tiger's nature is not compatible with people's nature since tigers love to eat people."

Ali, by his selection of friends over the course of his professional life, did prove that he didn't hate white people. But he also showed an attitude that was typical of many Nation of Islam members: a willingness to formally withdraw from the quest to integrate. In the late sixties, blacks in the lowest economic classes, which made up the overwhelming majority of Nation of Islam members, had very little meaningful contact with whites. To most black Muslims, separation was merely speaking the truth about what was happening and lacked *practical* meaning. If a black man worked for a white man and had no social contact with him, was never invited to his home or to his church, then why should he not formalize the arrangement by calling it separation? If a black man's life was not considered valuable to whites, then why should he seek to integrate?

In 1967, rioting resulted in eighty-two deaths, thousands injured, and 18,000 blacks arrested throughout the United States. There was a costly war going on while the inner cities were crumbling. It was a familiar scene to the African-American author James Baldwin, who wrote, "Everything was falling down and going to pieces. And no one cared. And it spelled out to me with brutal clarity and in every possible way that I was a worthless human being."

The Kerner Commission, established in August 1967 to investigate the riots across the country, concluded in a report dated March 2, 1968, that America was headed for two separate nations, one white and the other black. The FBI started tracking Ali's movements and listening to his phone calls. His speeches were recorded and his associates noted.

But while Ali was being attacked in the press for spreading hate and being against the war, the country was seeing an outpouring of rage against blacks. On April 4, 1968, on the balcony of the Lorraine Motel in Memphis, Tennessee, Dr. Martin Luther King, Jr., was assassinated. King, an advocate of integration and a man who pleaded for acceptance of all people regardless of skin color, who advocated nonviolence, was brutally gunned down. The Nation of Islam, who had so often disagreed with King's strategies, now pointed to his murder as proof of the mayhem that was being loosed on the black community. On June 5, 1968, only three months after the death of Dr. Martin Luther King, Jr., came the assassination in Los Angeles of Robert Kennedy, who had often championed black causes.

All the while, many young white Americans were fleeing to Canada to escape the draft. Others went to jail rather than fight in a war that was increasingly being questioned. The grim statistics coming from the military showed large numbers of men being killed and wounded in a seemingly endless escapade. The United States had been involved, first as advisers and then as combatants, in Vietnam since 1954, and the body count was piling up.

In December 1968, Ali was arrested for driving without a valid license in Dade County, Florida. He was jailed for nearly a week in what appeared to be a purely vindictive exercise.

With the murder of Dr. Martin Luther King, Jr., more blacks than ever lost faith in the willingness of the United States to grant them the rights of full citizenship. At the 1968 summer Olympics in Mexico, two black sprinters raised their fists in the black power salute while on the medals stand during "The Star-Spangled Banner." If America wanted business as usual, it wasn't going to get it.

Ali's appearances at college campuses were increasingly popular. What he was saying made more and more sense to his young audiences. America needed to be out of Vietnam. America needed to deal with racism. America needed to get onto a moral path.

Could Ali lead black America? He lacked the education and sophistication to assume a national role, but he was a clear thinker and many of his views would one day be accepted. The truth of the matter was that with the death of Dr. Martin Luther King, Jr., the voice of nonviolence and of moderation, black leadership was in a crisis. Compared with the Black Panthers, the 5 Percenters, a black radical group, and the emerging Symbionese Liberation Army, the Nation of Islam was becoming the voice of moderation.

In December 1969, Ali appeared in *Big Time Buck White,* a Broadway play in which he did some singing as well as acting. His reviews were generally quite good. The mood toward him was changing enough to present him before middle- and upper-class America. Promoters realized it was time to get him back into boxing.

In fact, there was no legal basis for keeping Ali out of boxing. While the World Boxing Association could strip him of its title, they could not stop him from fighting outside of their association. The ban on Ali was a "gentlemen's agreement" in some cases and political pressure in others. In those states with State Athletic Commissions it was necessary to have a state-granted license to fight — a license that could be denied Ali on the grounds that he had been convicted of a crime. With the pressure lessening, promoters put together a fight pitting Muhammad Ali, now twenty-eight, against a talented twenty-five-year-old Irish-American named Jerry Quarry.

Where, two and a half years earlier, prominent blacks had distanced themselves from Ali, they now flocked to this first fight after his exile. Coretta Scott King was there, as were actors Bill Cosby and Sidney Poitier. From Atlanta were the activists Ralph Abernathy, Julian Bond, and Andrew Young.

Ali, in his exile, had become a symbol of defiance against the American power structure. He had taken their best shot, and he was still standing. Still standing, but the fight was not over yet. His conviction continued to make its way through the court system. If all of the appeals were denied, he would still have to serve the five-year sentence handed down to him in 1967.

Jerry Quarry was a fighter who had likely experienced more poverty than Ali had. Quarry knew he was fighting for his future. His wasn't a fight of white against black. He could either be a mere statistic on Ali's comeback trail, or give himself the possibility of millions with a win.

It was fitting that Atlanta, with its affluent black population, would be the site of Ali's comeback. Few American cities had as much black political clout or savvy. Moreover, dozens of black celebrities, even those who had shunned Ali a few years earlier, were eager to welcome him back to public acceptance. America had radically changed since

Ali's banishment in 1967, and more and more people found Ali's views less bothersome. In 1967 he had spoken out against the war in Vietnam. By 1970 many Americans were wondering what we were doing in Southeast Asia. In 1967 Ali had upset many blacks by speaking for separation of the races while Dr. Martin Luther King, Jr., had spoken so eloquently for integration, but King's death at the hands of a white assassin made even the middle class wonder if integration was worth the struggle. Finally, Ali had conducted himself admirably during his years of exile, representing himself as a strong black man with no animosity for any other race. Black Atlantans came out to root for Ali in this match against a good white fighter.

The first round saw the old Ali, on his toes, moving, jabbing, throwing combinations — in a word, pretty. The second round saw a different Ali. The nervous energy was gone, and the legs that had danced in the first round began to shuffle. Quarry, a solid boxer who had won the heavyweight division of the Golden Gloves in 1965, slowed Ali down even more with punishing body blows in the second round. Tony Perez, the referee, thought that Ali might be beaten. The Atlanta crowd tensed as the victory they had come to see was in doubt.

The third round came, and Ali was again flat-footed. The quick feet and nimble legs that had kept him out of trouble as Cassius Clay were now betraying him. Quarry

sensed it, too, and became more aggressive. Then Ali hit Quarry with a flurry of punches, opening up a large gash over his eye. When the round ended, Quarry's cornermen worked feverishly to close the cut.

Doctors should be in attendance at all fights, and they should be close to ringside, waiting to be called. Ali had insisted on black doctors at the fight, but Quarry had objected. As a result, there was a delay while a white doctor was located. Perez, the referee, had to make the call whether or not to let Quarry continue the fight when he saw that the cut was still open and bleeding.

"I'd never seen a cut like that before," he said. "You - could see the bone."

Perez stopped the fight, giving the decision to Ali on a technical knockout. Quarry's trainer thought it was the right decision. Quarry was disappointed, but accepted the loss gracefully.

Muhammad Ali was back.

THE CRUELEST SPORT

In the sixties and seventies the big money didn't come easy for the young fighter. A "club" fighter, one of the veterans who fought on a regular schedule, might earn a steady $200 or $300 a month, but rarely more. It wasn't until they fought the top tier of fighters that they could even expect to make enough to look forward to the payday. The typical young fighter had to have a day job to support himself and to buy the equipment he needed to fight — gloves, tapes, trunks, a robe, protective gear for the groin, sparring gloves, towels, protective headgear for amateur matches and sparring, and mouthpieces. He had to pay dues at a gym and for the time of a trainer, if he had one.

If and when a fighter turns professional, his finances are largely dependent on his management. Somebody has to arrange the fights and make an agreement with another manager as to the fight conditions and money. A representative fight for a young man just turning professional will be a four- or six-round fight against somebody with similar experience. The "purse," or payment for the fight, can be as little as $100 or less. While the money is virtually nonexistent for amateur and beginning professional fights, the punches are just as real.

Even when a fighter turns professional and is good, there is no reason to believe he will get the kinds of fights that will offer him a large purse. Fighters and their managers form a team that competes for purses and titles. A good young fighter, someone with the skills to be matched with the better fighters and therefore get more money, will simply be avoided by the other fighter-management teams. The object of pro boxing is not to win matches, but to make money. Why should a manager at the lower levels of boxing sign his fighter to a match he might lose? Good fighters who are not well connected with a management team can be on the shelf for years waiting for a chance that will never come. One way to get around this is for the fighter to draw attention to himself during his amateur career by winning either a Golden Gloves championship or a medal in the Olympics.

Charles "Sonny" Liston won the Golden Gloves heavyweight crown in 1953. Ernest Terrell won the championship in 1957. Jerry Quarry was a Golden Gloves champ in 1965. Muhammad Ali won both the Golden Gloves championship and the Olympic gold medal in 1960. And, in 1964 the heavyweight Olympic champion was a young fighter out of Philadelphia named Joe Frazier.

Even a major amateur title doesn't guarantee financial success in the professional ranks. However, thanks to his charisma and popularity, one of Ali's major influences on the sport was on the income of fighters. He attracted crowds, television viewers, and most importantly, advertisers.

A typical "gate," or profit from ticket sales, for a championship fight might be estimated at $500,000. One fighter, the star attraction, might get as much as 50 percent of the gate while the other fighter might sign for 20 percent. The other 30 percent went to the owners of the facility and the fight promoters. When the fight was over and the actual gate was counted up, minus expenses, the money realized might be as little as $200,000. The main attraction would then get 50 percent, or $100,000. Out of this money he would have to pay his management team as much as half, and he'd have to cover all of his own expenses. If he cleared $20,000 or so, he was lucky.

The fighter who signed for the lesser amount might end up with as little as $5,000. Not much payment for spending an evening in a ring with a man trying to knock you senseless.

One of the cruel aspects of boxing to this day is the reporting of incomes. Very often contracts offering a percentage of the gate wildly overestimate the anticipated income. This is done to build excitement for the fight. It's clearly desirable for a promoter, trying to attract viewers, to say that the fighters are vying for so many millions of dollars — a typical figure is $9 million to the champion, and $5.5 million to the challenger. This is usually a nonsense figure, but newspapers traditionally report it as if it were real.

Muhammad Ali, with his flamboyant style, his charm, and even the controversy swirling around him, brought a new level of interest to the sport and dramatically changed the income levels of boxing matches. He did this by a deep understanding of the media. Before Ali, fighters did not speak, they were spoken for. Few fight fans who lived during the era of Joe Louis could ever quote the man who had held the championship for so many years. What fans knew about Louis they learned from reporters. But Ali used the media to promote his bouts and himself. It was the new media, television and its sponsors, that provided the increased revenue that all fighters could hope for in the future.

Also, Ali had a unique insight into one popular aspect of boxing. Fighters often saw themselves as very macho, and the fight business as a sport for men of their kind. Ali looked at boxing as pure entertainment. His antics were those of an entertainer, and he knew exactly what he was doing with them. He brought people around him who had entertainment value to the media, including Drew "Bundini" Brown, with whom he would stand toe-to-toe and shout his "Float like a butterfly, sting like a bee" slogan. He hired an ailing Stepin Fetchit, the black entertainer, as a handyman around his camp. Even Ali's relationship with the press was that of an entertainer. He avoided those reporters who kept trying to pry for insights into his relationship with the Nation of Islam. But reporters who appreciated Ali's entertainment value were allowed in his camp. In particular, the sports television journalist Howard Cosell admired Ali as an athlete and embraced his antics, and the two men became close friends.

Muhammad Ali made more money than any other boxer in history. He also allowed the fighters he faced in the ring to make more money than they could have even dreamed of without him. Ironically, many of them didn't realize this fact.

Each time a fighter steps into the ring he knows there will be a cost. For the glory of the possible win there will be a price measured in units of pain. He will have an idea, if he is honest with himself, of just how much pain he will have to endure on a given night, how much blood he will lose, and just how long it will take for his body to recover from the inevitable battering. Every fight hurts. Every fight damages the body. Some damage the soul.

Fights are often decided in the dressing room as the fighter extends his imagination to the glare of ringside. The image of the impending battle flickers through his mind, and he visualizes himself winning, punishing his

opponent more than he is punished. He sees himself using his style, using those tools most comfortable to him, to control the fight. Muhammad Ali could see himself moving quickly, throwing out lightning jabs, leaning back, just out of the reach of the desperate hooks. He saw himself frustrating his opponent, imposing his will on the fight. But even if he was convinced that he could win the fight, convinced beyond the hype and the false bravado he offered to the press, he must still have assessed how much suffering he could bear to carry it off.

When the pain comes, it can be excruciating. A two hundred-pound heavyweight at the top of his form can deliver a devastating blow. A good single blow to the face can break the neck of an ordinary person. Those watching on television or at ringside can scream at a fighter who lies helplessly against the ropes or who has stumbled heavily to the canvas, to get back into the fight. But few fight fans have ever been hit with even a glancing blow from a real fighter. They don't know the courage it takes to continue when the body is screaming to give it up.

Body punches bruise the muscles that help a fighter turn and lift his arms. They push the ribs out of shape; they bruise and tear the internal organs. Hours after the fight the torn tissue and bleeding show up as a bloody tint in the urine.

A fighter's head throbs. Cuts are alive with pain as they are slammed again and again or as a glove is scraped across the exposed nerves. Forehead cuts bleed into the eyes and give color to the violence. Fighters hurt. They survive by accepting the agony of fighting as a way of life.

In the top ranks there are trainers and doctors at ringside, and other doctors to examine and care for the boxer. At the lower end of the spectrum there is less medical attention, less time to heal between fights, less money for good treatment.

Whether the medical treatment received before and after a fight is good or bad, the damage to the body is still done. Mostly, the body is forgiving. It will usually heal. The major physical problems that fighters encounter are with the eyes and with the brain. Physicians have long studied the effects of fighting, and especially of taking blows to the head. Some feel that boxing can be made safer. Others disagree: They feel that as long as the aim of professional fighting is to do damage to the head and body, it will be a dangerous sport. Just how destructive is fighting to the human body? Doctors debate, but fighters know.

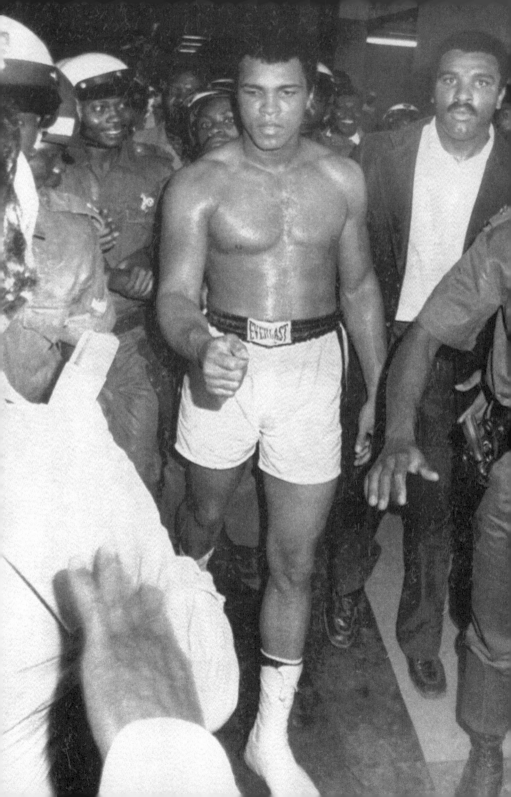

Part III

THE PEOPLE'S CHAMPION

I got a surprise for Clay   He's the greatest, the biggest in everything he does, and no man can be all those things. He loudmouthed so long and bigtalked so much that he got himself in a box. You know what I mean? The man has to do or die. I think he's going to die.

— Joe Frazier, *Sports Illustrated*, February 22, 1971

And it came to pass, when he had made an end of speaking, that he cast away the jawbone out of his hand . . .

— Judges 15:17

ALI VS. FRAZIER

If there is such a thing as a stereotypical fighter, it was Joe Frazier. Born into a dirt-poor family in Beaufort, South Carolina, on January 12, 1944, Joe had moved to Philadelphia and an amateur boxing career by his mid teens. The inner-city streets of Philadelphia are brutally tough, and the fighters that come from the area are known for an aggressive, bruising style. In 1964, Frazier came to national attention by winning the Olympic heavyweight championship.

Frazier, a compact five feet eleven, was a "busy" fighter, coming after an opponent relentlessly, head bobbing, moving into the action, always trying to set up his powerful left hook. His style was simple: He inflicted brutal punishment on any fighter he faced. If his opponent were a wall, he would knock down the wall. If his opponent were a mountain, he would knock down the mountain. Like all champions, he worked hard in training. When other fighters trained by sparring three rounds a day, Frazier would spar eight. He also maintained a steady job, working in a slaughterhouse, to support his family.

Smokin' Joe, as he was known, turned professional in 1965. He won four fights in that year and nine the next, scoring four one-round knockouts. By the end of 1967, with Muhammad Ali out of boxing, Frazier was considered to be the number one contender for the heavyweight championship. In March 1968, he defeated Buster Mathis, a tall, lumbering fighter, and was crowned heavyweight champion.

What Frazier wanted from boxing was to make a living, but he also wanted to be part of a tradition that had taken poor black men from southern farms and city ghettos to the big time. Fighting on a championship level meant good money, but it also meant a kind of respect that a black man with little education couldn't get anywhere else. It meant having your picture taken with celebrities, and signing autographs. It meant having reporters ask you questions about topics they wouldn't have dreamed of discussing with you if you hadn't been the champion. It meant being called "champ" instead of "boy."

"It's like a fraternity," Jimmy Dupree, former light heavyweight contender and trainer observed. "You get initiated in the wars you fight with somebody as good or better than you. Then you learn who you really are deep inside. After you've been through those wars, and you still have the heart to continue in this game, you're in the fraternity and everybody else that knows what those wars are about owe you respect."

When Frazier assumed the championship in March 1968, however, a huge shadow hung over his title. That shadow was Muhammad Ali. It was Ali people were still talking about. Ali had beaten the fearsome Liston, the reigning champion, twice. He had also beaten and humiliated the former champion, Floyd Patterson. He was still the star the reporters were going to for interviews. He was still claiming the championship that had been taken from him by the World Boxing Association.

After the March fight that earned him the championship, Frazier went back into the ring two more times in 1968. The first fight was against Manuel Ramos, whom he stopped in two rounds on June 24. The second fight was a December 10 decision against Oscar Bonavena, a rugged if uninspired fighter from South America. Neither fight attracted much attention. To make matters worse, there was a dispute over who exactly owned the championship. The New York State Athletic Commission claimed it was Frazier, but the competing World Boxing Association disputed the claim and had their own box-off, eventually naming Jimmy Ellis, from Louisville, as their champion.

In 1969 there were only two fights for Frazier: one against Dave Zyglewicz on April 22, in which Frazier scored a first-round knockout, and the other against Jerry Quarry on June 23. There was little to gain for Frazier in the fight against Zyglewicz, an unknown who had practically no drawing power.

A white contender would have attracted attention by bringing more white fans to the arenas. People who - weren't fight fans needed to identify with the fighters before they would purchase seats to watch the bouts. Quarry, a good, tough boxer, was just below the championship level in skills and stamina. He had the courage, but had a tendency to get cut badly. Boxing, without a major personality, is not a very lucrative sport.

To their credit, Frazier's handlers did not try to get him a lot of low-level fights. The fight game was about money, and there was no reason for Joe to risk himself if the money wasn't there. Meanwhile, a number of fighters were being touted as possible contenders for the throne that Ali had vacated, virtually ignoring Frazier. Even when Frazier defeated Jimmy Ellis in February 1970, uniting the two championships (the New York State Athletic Commission and the World Boxing Association), there was still little interest in the talented but colorless Philadelphian. But rumors had it that Muhammad Ali was going to be allowed to fight again. There was still opposition, opposition that included such high-powered names as Senator Strom Thurmond and Ronald Reagan, then governor of California. But in October 1970, a deal was worked out in Atlanta when Ali was signed to fight Jerry Quarry. A month later Frazier fought and knocked out a good light heavyweight, Bob Foster. In December of the same year, Ali wore down a determined Oscar Bonavena. Ali and Frazier had fought and defeated the same two fighters, Quarry and Bonavena. All the talk was for a match between Ali and Frazier. The match for the world heavyweight title was set for March 8, 1971, in New York City.

"Come on up, work hard, and I'll make you rich," Ali had said to Frazier after the 1964 Olympics.

The two men knew each other. Frazier, two years younger, understood that Ali would be the man to beat. He had seen Ali's fights; he knew what he could do. He had also respected Ali, even when fighters like Floyd Patterson were jumping on the anti-Muslim bandwagon. Ali, on the other hand, couldn't stand the idea that prominent black men chose to be "nonpolitical." He bad-mouthed Frazier in public, saying that Joe didn't stand up for the black man, that he was an "Uncle Tom" — a black who went along with whites to be accommodating. Ali was setting himself up as the true black champion while Frazier was, at best, a pretender who did not deserve the support of black people.

Ali's taunts, the same ones he used against Liston and Patterson, bothered Joe Frazier more than the other fighters. To Liston, Ali was just annoying. Patterson's dislike for Ali was based on his idea of what Ali represented. But Liston and Patterson had already gained their championships and their places in history when they first ran into Ali. Liston was the menacing thug, the baddest man in the house, a role he relished. Patterson was Mr. Nice Guy, a likable man with excellent skills. Frazier was still fighting for respect. He didn't like it when Ali called him ugly or stupid. He also didn't like the idea that Ali was violating a basic concept of fighting: to always show respect for your opponent.

Monday night, March 8, 1971: This was the night that fight fans around the world were waiting for. For many African Americans it was to be the night when the man who personified "Black is Beautiful" would regain the championship. For Joe Frazier this would be the night, finally, when he would gain the world's respect.

At ringside, Hugh McIlvanney, covering the fight for the British press, noted how many white American reporters were openly hostile to Ali. Everyone understood one thing: Ali had never faced a fighter with the skills and determination of Smokin' Joe Frazier.

The fight started with the two men both working comfortably in their styles. Frazier moving, bobbing, relentlessly aggressive. Ali jabbed and moved, jabbed and moved, floated like a butterfly, stung like a bee. Frazier had predicted that Ali would have no chance to slug it out with him toe-to-toe and would understand that.

"He's going to have to do two things, move backward and fight," Frazier said. "I only have to fight."

Ali moved backward, fighting in flurries that made Fra-

zier look hopelessly outclassed. But Frazier did not fall —
he kept on coming. Occasionally Ali would tie him up
and talk to him, as if he were utterly disdainful of Joe's
talents. Still, Frazier kept coming. When Ali tried to lie
against the ropes, Frazier punished his body with blows
that sometimes landed against the hips and thighs of the
taller man. In the center of the ring Frazier made sure that
Ali had no time to rest.

For the first nine rounds it looked as if Ali could simply
cruise through the fight, popping away at Frazier at will.
Then, in the tenth and eleventh rounds, Ali began to slow,
as he had done in the Quarry and Bonavena fights. The
difference was in the fighter he was now facing. A left
hook caught Ali and sent him reeling toward the ropes.
He clutched and held on, smothering Frazier's onslaught
with ring savvy. The crowd sensed that Frazier was coming on.

The fight was scheduled for fifteen rounds, and it
looked as if it would only be a matter of time until Frazier
got to Ali for the knockout. Among the press, Ali's detractors were now screaming for Frazier to destroy "The
Greatest."

The fourteenth round. Ali summoned up a new reserve
of strength. For a brief time he brought the fight back
to his style, jabbing, moving, hitting Frazier with right
crosses that would have knocked down a less game fighter.
At the end of the round both fighters, close to their physical limits, went wearily back to their corners.

The outcome of the fight was still in doubt. It looked like Frazier was winning, but was he? How were the early rounds scored? Could Ali be ahead? Both fighters were told that they needed the final round.

Frazier had come too far to back down. He had trained too long and worked too hard to concede even a moment of the fight. Ali moved for the first seconds of the round, but the fabulous legs soon grew heavy, and he was leaning against the ropes and trying to tie Joe up. The speed was gone and the last round was all Frazier, capped by a thunderous left hook to Ali's jaw that sent him to the canvas. Ali got up quickly. He had survived Frazier's final onslaught, but there was no doubt who had won the fight.

It was Muhammad Ali's first professional defeat.

The world had seen a magnificent bout conducted by two great fighters. They had seen Joe Frazier take everything that Muhammad Ali could dish out and still maintain his style. As he predicted, Ali had to do two things, move backward and fight. All Frazier had to do was fight.

They had also seen Muhammad Ali take more punishment than ever before. His speed was no longer as reliable as it had been. Ali, sitting dejectedly in the locker room, his jaw swollen from the impact of Frazier's blow, seemed suddenly mortal.

If the sportswriters who had urged Frazier to slaughter Ali thought that the defeat had put an end to his popularity, they were wrong. Ali came out of the fight with more fans than ever. The glee that some sportswriters dis-

Next page: The March 1971 fight against Joe
Frazier—Ali's first professional defeat.

93

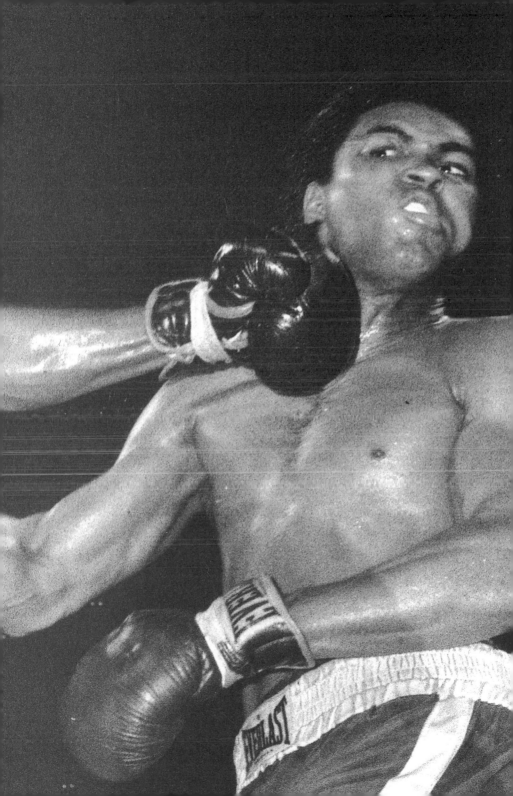

played in their dispatches following the fight served only to strengthen the resolve of Ali's fans, especially young - people throughout the world, to continue supporting him. Muhammad Ali, labeled by some the champion of the Black Muslims, was still the people's champion.

COMEBACK

Ali had lost to Joe Frazier, but, to many, he was still champion. For young people he was the voice that spoke against Vietnam when thousands of their brothers were dying in a war that few understood. He was the voice of youth as no other boxer had ever been — brash, outspoken, courageous. Ali, even into his thirties, looked younger than other fighters. Fighters often size each other up, trying to read beyond the physical bulk of other men, trying to see what kind of heart is beating beneath the muscled chest. Ali, with his young face and expressive eyes, had the kind of looks with which even the mildest man could identify.

But while many whites embraced Ali as a man of his times, both entertaining and symbolic of the growing importance of youth to America, to blacks he was special for deeper reasons. If black was truly beautiful, it was Muhammad Ali, in his form and in his style, who personified that beauty. If blacks were tired of taking the back-seat, Ali was the one showing them the way to the front seat. Ali was turning young black America away from begging for their rights, and enduring the insults of those hostile to equal rights, to a bold new position that depended more on the inner strengths of the black community.

Joe Frazier, on the other hand, was like the good father in so many black families. He did his job well and with dignity. He took care of business. But Smokin' Joe, like so many black men before him, seemed restricted in his scope and his promise. He was understood and respected in the black community, but was not the model young - people wished to copy.

Ali's assertiveness, his ability to confront authority as few blacks had ever publicly done, was what young African Americans wanted to emulate. His confidence in his abilities was a goal that had eluded black youth. But he had lost against Joe Frazier, and that defeat was a loss for the Nation of Islam as well as for the fighter from Louisville.

It was 1971, and both Malcolm X and Dr. Martin Luther King, Jr., had been assassinated, and there was confusion as to just how the civil rights movement would proceed. Richard Nixon was president, and the movement seemed stalled. The National Association for the Advancement of Colored People, or NAACP, was less than active, and Elijah Muhammad, now in his seventies, was no longer the dynamic leader he had been. The deaths of Malcolm X and King had also discouraged a lot of black people. Both assassinations still had unresolved questions that indicated black leadership could easily be pushed aside. Ali had not been a leader of the black community, but he was a strong and effervescent personality around which young people could rally.

The question was, would Muhammad Ali ever be the champion again? Red Smith, one of the nation's most respected sportswriters and a vehement Ali detractor, predicted that if Ali fought Frazier a dozen times, he would lose a dozen times.

Ali had to accept what all fighters eventually have to deal with — the idea that being beaten was possible. He realized two things in the decisive loss to Frazier: The speed he had enjoyed before his layoff had lessened; and there would always be strong young fighters, fighters with skill and courage, to challenge him.

His detractors gloated at his loss. Joe Frazier was invited to speak before the South Carolina legislature, not for his win over Muhammad Ali, a fellow fighter, but for his win over Muhammad Ali, the fighter who dared the world to deal with his blackness.

Ali had always been close to his mother, and his brother was perhaps his best friend in the world. After his loss to Frazier he found himself trying to cheer up his mother and having quiet talks with his younger brother who looked up to him so much. There was always a distance between Ali and his father, and few words were passed between them after the Frazier fight.

Ali respected Frazier's ability and began to think about a comeback. He knew the young Ali would not have been hit nearly as often as he had been in the loss to Frazier. If fighting was a matter of imposing one style over the other, could changing his style help him prevail against the young, up-and-coming fighters?

Ali's legal status, the most important fight of his life, was resolved on June 28, 1971. On that day the Supreme Court of the United States unanimously reversed Ali's conviction on refusing induction. The Court found that, in refusing Ali's petition for conscientious objector status, the draft board had failed to specify which of its conditions the fighter had failed to meet. Since the government had conceded in its argument before the Supreme Court that Ali had met two of the tests — that his opposition was based on his religious training as a Muslim and that he was sincere in his beliefs — a denial that could have been based on either of these two would have been wrong. By using the technical flaw in the draft board's decision rather than the parameters of the status itself, the Court allowed the conviction to be overturned without allowing a blanket ruling which would have made all members of the Nation of Islam eligible for CO status. Ali, now approaching his thirtieth birthday and past his physical prime, began the climb back to the championship.

Ali's first fight after Frazier was against Jimmy Ellis, his friend and sparring partner from Louisville. They had fought together since they were kids — there was nothing

Ali could do that Ellis did not know. Ellis was a good boxer with a strong left jab. What he feared about Ali was a right hand over that jab. They fought a number of fairly even rounds until Ali, anticipating the jab, timed it perfectly and countered with the right hand that Ellis knew would come. Ali had won. The fight was stopped in the twelfth round on a technical knockout.

The next fight was held in Houston, Texas, against Buster Mathis. Mathis had beaten Joe Frazier in the Olympic trials but injured himself shortly before he was to participate in the 1964 Games. He was the heaviest of the heavyweights, with bulk that placed between 260 and 300 pounds on his six foot, three inch frame. Mathis had good foot and hand speed but was an average puncher. He was also not dedicated to a training regime, which was evident in his inconsistent performances. Ali fought Mathis in November 1971. The sluggish Mathis was an easy target, and Ali took an easy decision. However, the same sportswriters who had lambasted Ali for beating Ernie Terrell without mercy in 1967, now chided him for going light on Mathis. Ali knew that his performances in the ring, no matter how good they were, would not please his enemies.

Boxing fans around the world were eager to see Ali and offered better purses than were available at home. Ali fought Mac Foster in Tokyo in April 1972, winning by a lackluster decision in fifteen rounds.

On the first day of May, exactly a month after the Foster fight, Ali fought a twelve-rounder with George Chuvalo in Vancouver, British Columbia. He won this fight by decision, and there was more talk that he had lost the fire necessary to regain his top form. But Ali had, at this time, fought 108 amateur fights and 37 professional fights. He had been in the professional fight game for almost twelve years, and even his magnificent body could not perform as it once had.

In June 1972, he fought a rematch with Jerry Quarry, this time stopping Quarry in seven rounds. Less than a month later he faced Al "Blue" Lewis in Dublin, Ireland. An easy win was predicted, and Ali fulfilled it, winning on a technical knockout in eleven rounds.

There were two more fights for Ali in 1972, each of them significant in their own way. The first was yet another fight against Floyd Patterson. Nobody expected Patterson to win. The fight, however, was significant for Patterson and, in a way, for Joe Frazier as well. During his usual pre-fight boasting, Ali once again denigrated Patterson, the man who once claimed he wanted to "destroy" Ali because of his ties to the Nation of Islam. In a long article written by Milton Gross and published in *Sports Illustrated*, Patterson was quoted as having said that Ali was a disgrace to boxing and to his race. Ali's subsequent open humiliation of Patterson was a violation of the unwritten rule of the fight game — that fighters show at least public respect for other professional fighters. In the macho world of boxing, honor was everything and Ali took away that honor from Patterson, beating him convincingly in seven rounds. It was true that many of the black fighters Ali faced had joined the chorus of white sportswriters who had put Ali down when he joined the Nation of Islam and refused to serve in the army. The articles they allowed to be printed in their names, and the statements they made against Ali destroyed any remnant of respect he might have had for them. Ali was a political man, and his political stance was largely based on the history of the black man in America.

The fight with Bob Foster on November 21, 1972, was an important chapter in Ali's comeback. Foster was a light heavyweight who had put on enough pounds to qualify as a heavyweight. As a light heavyweight he had been fast and had a good punch. Foster's handlers thought that Ali might have deteriorated enough for Foster to win. Ali won the fight on a knockout in the eighth round, but not before Foster had inflicted enough damage on Ali to claim that the fight had been close up to the knockout. The reaction of boxing insiders was unanimous: Ali's days of being a top contender were numbered. At thirty, Ali could not survive the ring wars for very long.

If 1972 was a lackluster year for Ali, 1973 was a disaster. He fought Joe Bugner on February 14 in Las Vegas. The most notable event of the fight was Ali's new robe, a gift from Elvis Presley, upon which was emblazoned PEOPLE'S CHAMPION.

Next page: Ali vs. Floyd Patterson, September 20, 1972.

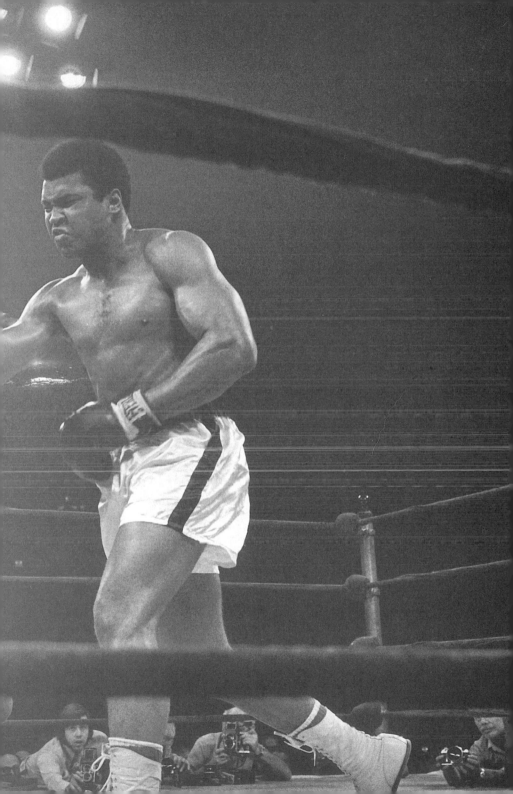

Then came the fight against Ken Norton on March 31 in San Diego. Norton, a former sparring partner of Ali's, was given little chance. A plodding, heavily muscled man, he had the kind of defensive style that always bothered Ali. In the second round, Ali, in typical fashion, leaned back from a punch. Norton's follow-up punch landed hard on Ali's jaw, breaking the bone. At first his cornermen didn't realize the extent of his injury. Ali didn't want the fight stopped. The pain was agonizing, and the fight was scheduled for twelve long rounds.

The Norton fight marked another display of Muhammad Ali's tremendous courage. It took courage just to walk into a ring knowing that someone was waiting to hurt him, waiting to beat him senseless. It took courage for Ali to face Sonny Liston as a twenty-two-year-old, and to announce after the fight that he had joined the Nation of Islam with their separatist policies.

When he refused induction into the armed forces, he knew he might very well go to prison. It didn't make any difference what the rules were. He was a black man standing up to the authorities. Now, with his skills clearly failing him, it took courage to not fold against Norton.

When the final round started, one judge had Ali ahead by two points, another had Norton ahead by a point, and the third had the fight even. Norton dominated the final round against a tired and hurt Ali, and was declared the winner. After the fight, Ali was taken to the hospital, where he underwent ninety minutes of surgery to repair the jaw that had been broken clean through.

Sportswriters for the *New York Post* celebrated the victory. At last Ali was getting beaten. Even though he was considered past his prime, it still made some people feel good to see him lose.

Ali couldn't fight again until September. He was matched again with Norton. The fight was as close as it had been the first time around, but Ali had come into the bout in much better physical condition, and was able to rally to beat Norton in the twelfth round.

A month later Ali's fight year ended with an easy win over Rudi Lubbers in Jakarta, Indonesia.

Ali forged on with his comeback against the backdrop of three major events in 1973. One was the cease-fire in Vietnam. The war had been an unbelievable drain on American resources, and the reasons for the war seemed more and more distant and unclear. America, the strongest nation on the earth, had completely lost its direction. The cease-fire sought to get American troops out of Vietnam with dignity. The North Vietnamese understood that America was tired of the war, that they were the ones winning the war of attrition, not the larger nation. The cease-fire negotiations were not successful, and the war began anew.

The second major event was the Watergate scandal. For the first time in modern history a president of the United

States was being investigated by the American judicial system. During 1973, White House aides resigned, the attorney general was indicted, and there was talk of impeaching President Richard Nixon.

A third event, far less important to those outside the boxing world, was the two-round knockout of Joe Frazier by George Foreman on January 22 in Kingston, Jamaica.

In other times in the long history of boxing, the natural consequence of Frazier's loss of the championship would have been a rematch between Frazier and Foreman. But past his prime or not, it was Ali who was still the driving force in boxing. Ali had expanded his own visibility far beyond that of any other fighter who had ever lived. He had made albums, he had been in a play on Broadway (*Big Time Buck White*), in a comic book (*Muhammad Ali vs. Superman*), and had even had his image on a shoe polish container. He had appeared hundreds of times on television and had been interviewed in dozens of magazines. He had spoken on college campuses throughout the country, and had been seen with leaders from around the world. Foreman, the new champion, was best known for his 1968 Olympic victory. Another Ali-Frazier fight was scheduled for New York's Madison Square Garden on January 28, 1974.

SMOKIN' JOE VS. THE LEGEND

Had Joe Frazier been so badly beaten in the first match against Ali that he did not want a rematch? On both sides of the Atlantic rumors circulated about Frazier's deteriorating physical condition. He had fought and defeated Muhammad Ali in March 1971, and did not fight the rest of the year while Ali fought three times. In 1972, Frazier took on Terry Daniels in New Orleans, and later, in Omaha, Nebraska, Ron Stander. Neither of these fighters were of the first rank and neither offered Smokin' Joe anywhere near the kind of money he would make in a match with Ali.

There were rumors of contract negotiations breaking down, of Joe not wanting to give Ali another chance at the championship, and of delaying the fight for tax reasons. None of these held water. In reality, both fighters were past their physical prime. The punishing physical wear and tear of professional boxing was appalling, and both fighters were showing the unmistakable signs of damage.

Black men suffer from hypertension, or high blood pressure, more than any other people in the world. Within the African-American community it is one of the leading causes of death of men over thirty. Joe Frazier had a serious problem with hypertension. His blood pressure had been high enough to threaten disqualification.

Frazier's two-week stay in the hospital after the Ali fight was due largely to his hypertension, and not solely to the injuries he received during the fight. His high blood pressure stemmed not simply from the bout itself, but from the weeks and months of stress during training. The side-effects of medications for high blood pressure include weakness, and sometimes even dizziness when the body changes position rapidly. Frazier knew that another bout with Muhammad Ali would compel him to train hard enough to possibly do permanent damage to his blood vessels.

The fight against George Foreman on January 22, 1973, in Kingston, Jamaica, was a disaster for Frazier. Before the fight he was scarcely recognized as the world's heavyweight champion — that title was still largely associated with Muhammad Ali.

The two-round knockout at the hands of George Foreman stunned the boxing world. Foreman had not been an impressive fighter prior to the Frazier fight. In 1968 he had won the Olympic gold medal in Mexico City, standing out by waving a small American flag in contrast to other black athletes raising black-gloved hands in protest against what they felt to be the racism in their own country. His match with Frazier was turning out to be just another payday until one of his thunderous right hands knocked Smokin' Joe loose from the title.

After being defeated by Foreman, Frazier went a full twelve rounds with Joe Bugner in London in July 1973. The rematch with Ali was arranged for the last Monday in January 1974. Monday night fights insured a large television audience. Theaters were running the fight closed-circuit, and sponsors were lining up with fists full of dollars.

The Ali-Frazier rematch was the fight sports fans wanted to see. There was no question that Frazier intensely disliked Ali, so there would be an air of vengeance about the match. Frazier had lost to Foreman, but by then Ali had shown signs of real slippage, losing to Norton once and barely beating him the second time.

At weigh-in, the two fighters were within a pound of each other, with Frazier, at 214, only a pound lighter than the taller Ali. Frazier had been six pounds lighter in their first match.

When fighters reach championship level they are excellent tacticians. They know what the man facing them is going to do, what his capabilities are, and they have strategies for putting up a good defense. The problem comes when a fighter is forced into a defense that prevents him from carrying out his offense. Just as Frazier had known that Ali would have to back up against him and use his hand speed to counterattack, Ali knew that Frazier would have to keep coming in and taking punches in order to begin his attack.

The fight started as predicted, with Ali moving backward, jabbing at the bobbing head before him, and tying Frazier up when Frazier moved inside Ali's longer reach. Frazier, for his part, moved from side to side, and threw bombs toward Ali's body. As the fight progressed there were subtle differences from the first encounter between the two men. Ali relied more on his jab, often landing high on Frazier's forehead, and rested less on the ropes. Frazier punished Ali's body, as he said he would, and threw fewer heavy punches toward Ali's head. In the late rounds, when Smokin' Joe had come on in so many fights, a tired Frazier began punching from long range, hoping to get lucky. Ali was the clear winner, though neither fighter was hurt as badly as in the first fight. But it was obvious that each fighter was older.

Was Ali back? Was he again the Ali who had been barred from boxing from twenty-five to twenty-eight, a fighter's peak performance years? People who should have known better declared that the real Ali had returned.

Who was the real Ali? Few people could claim to truly know the man. To begin to know Ali, one first had to know what it was like to be black in the American South before the civil rights movement. Cassius Clay, Sr., had learned his "place" as a black man. He had learned that his place was in the back of the bus and in the "colored" waiting room in the train station. He knew not to sit down in certain restaurants, and he knew that he would be addressed by his first name or be called "boy" until he was an old man, at which time he would be called "uncle."

The bus lines didn't run very regularly in the black sections of Louisville. Adults who had cars used them, and younger people, including Cassius Clay, rode bicycles. Riding a bicycle meant avoiding the humbling experience of having to sit in the back of buses.

In the fifties, Muhammad Ali had to balance the segregated South of his youth with the world of opportunity that boxing brought him. He had to discover which was real, and which existed for him only because he was the heavyweight champion of the world.

Ali had two sets of role models. One was that of the respectable fighters such as Joe Louis and Archie Moore. But Ali saw how America had treated Joe Louis. Louis had served in the army, had done the right thing, and yet had still been forced to fight long after his prime by a government not forgiving enough to see past his tax problems. Joe Louis had ended his career with a humiliating knockout at the hands of twenty-nine-year-old Rocky Marciano. Ali witnessed the end of Archie Moore's career and saw the ancient Archie climbing into the ring with men half his age.

After the 1968 Olympic protests, Jesse Owens, the spectacular sprinter from the 1936 games, was called to speak to the young black athletes. Ali saw pictures of Owens confronting the young black men, telling them that race had no business in the Olympics, only to have them counter with how America had quickly discarded the most exciting man in track and field after the Berlin games had finished.

Ali was a child of the television age. As television brought the Vietnam War and the civil rights movement into American homes, it also brought Muhammad Ali. If there was such a thing as a new breed of black man, Ali was its ideal. Blessed with talent and determination, he was the voice not only of young black men, but of young - people everywhere.

Ali was also of the generation that saw the assassinations of Americans who had stood up for humanity. John F. Kennedy. Malcolm X. Dr. Martin Luther King, Jr. Robert Kennedy. The four students protesting the war at Kent State University who were killed by National Guardsmen. Ali had spoken out against the war in Vietnam before it was politically correct to do so. And stood up for what he believed in and was willing to pay the price for his beliefs.

Above all, Ali was a fighter, and to the altar of his fame and fortune, he brought his body. He took the punishment, bore the pain when it was the only way he could win, and endured when others would have failed. He knew what that sacrifice meant. And he especially knew what it meant to stay in the game that had always been meant for younger, faster, stronger men.

Ali's next fight was scheduled for October 30, 1974. It would be held in Kinshasa, the capital of Zaire, in central Africa. Who was the real Ali? Once again, the world was about to find out.

RUMBLE IN THE JUNGLE

Muhammad Ali was no longer at the top of his game. He arrived in Zaire a fighter whose principal weapons, speed of foot and speed of hand, were failing him. Newspapers from around the world had sent reporters to the third largest country in Africa, many believing they had come to witness the demise of The Greatest.

George Foreman was twenty-five, a bull of a man who destroyed everything before him. Ali had struggled mightily against Norton, but Foreman had demolished him in only two rounds. Ali's battles with Joe Frazier had been classics of endurance, but Foreman had knocked Frazier senseless, again in two rounds. The promoters of the fight had convinced the government of Zaire to put up $10 million, $5 million for each fighter. It would be the greatest purse in ring history. Each fighter would be making more than stars like Joe Louis and Rocky Marciano had earned in their entire careers.

The entourage the promoters took to Africa to build the television interest included the soul singer James Brown, legendary blues man B. B. King, and a host of other African-American entertainers.

"How can he hit me when he can't catch me?" Muhammad Ali shouted to admiring crowds of Africans and reporters, throwing punches as he went backward around the practice ring in Zaire.

Big George Foreman practiced hitting the heavy bag. Writers Norman Mailer and George Plimpton watched as the young heavyweight champion punished the bag. They were awestruck at his power. Mailer, once an amateur boxer himself, noted the huge dents in the bag. Ali wasn't going to be doing much dancing if he got hit like that. Foreman practiced catching Ali. He brought in training partners who simulated Ali's quick movements. He practiced moving at angles around the square ring, a technique he would use to cut off Ali's escape routes.

Muhammad Ali was popular throughout Africa. He had traveled to Africa after first winning the heavyweight championship in 1964 and had been extensively profiled in the African press. A Zairean artist described him as being the one who "defended the good cause."

Foreman arrived stylishly dressed and lead a large German police dog. Zaire had been a former colony of

Belgium, and to the people of Kinshasa, police dogs were symbols of oppression. It was an unfortunate choice for Foreman, who wondered why Ali was so popular with the people. It was not Ali the fighter whom Zaireans admired, but Ali the man. They had read about Ali in international magazines, had seen him speaking up for black people in the United States, and had identified with him. In Ali they had a world-famous figure who was now mingling with their people, playing with their children in the streets of Kinshasa.

In Africa, Foreman became the brooding champion who had been deprived of the benefits of the championship. Ali had outshone Foreman as he had everyone else.

"Ali, bumbaye! Ali, bumbaye!" The crowd chanted whenever they saw Ali jogging along the highway. It meant, simply, "Ali, kill him!" Here were two black men, two men of African descent, fighting in Africa. But Ali was considered the real black champion, and the darker Foreman represented the enemy.

The documentary *When We Were Kings,* the story of the fight, was being filmed as the fight approached. On camera Foreman tried not to embarrass himself, tried to sound like a man of the world. Ali, seemingly born to excel in the new age of instant media, did much better. He was the articulate one, the one who would be quoted in the morning papers. "Black people in the United States don't know what Africa is like," he said. "And you people in Africa don't know anything about us. I need to change that."

The writers worked hard to make their prose distinctive. The entertainers worked to bring their talents to an appreciative African audience. The Africans, in turn, were eager to please and to learn from the Americans with their high technology and glitz. Don King, the slick talking, Shakespeare-quoting promoter, had put himself in the center of the match, hogging as much publicity for himself as possible. The match seemed at times to be an endless spectacle of entertainers and media; then there was a major setback.

During a session with a sparring partner, George Foreman was cut above the right eye. To have a cut that hadn't sufficiently healed and then face a boxer like Ali could easily have been the difference between winning and losing. The fight was postponed. The cut was treated, and the two fighters resumed training as they waited for Foreman to heal. The delay stretched to five weeks. All the hype settled down into an adventure with Third World facilities. The air-conditioning didn't work; communication with America and Europe via telephone didn't work; and there was also getting used to African food, African customs, and the lack of luxuries the Americans were used to having.

Wednesday, October 30, 1974. Finally, the morning of the rescheduled fight had arrived. It would begin at four o'clock in the morning to accommodate closed-circuit television in other parts of the world. Foreman was confident. He had Dick Sadler in his corner, one of the world's most respected trainers. He also had Archie Moore, who knew more about the fight game than anyone alive.

Angelo Dundee, in Ali's camp, was worried, but confident. Dundee still believed in his champion. How did Ali feel? Just before the Quarry comeback fight he had confessed to former champion Joe Louis that he was nervous. In Zaire he was nervous again. But he knew he would muster up the courage to go into the ring, and to do whatever it took to survive.

The time arrived. In Ali's dressing room there was dead silence.

"What are you people so unhappy about?" Ali asked.

They felt they were sending Ali out to his defeat. With his pride, Ali would not go down easy, and he might absorb the worst beating of his life. Ali began to lead his - people, people who had been with him for so many years — Angelo Dundee, Bundini Brown, Ali's brother Rahaman (formerly Rudolph Clay), masseuse Luis Sarria, and bodyguard Wali "Blood" Muhammad — in a cheerleading session.

"I'm going to dance!" Ali sang. "I'm going to dance!"

The chorus was a sad one, with some of the singers almost moved to tears. Norman Mailer, in Ali's dressing room, took deep breaths as the charismatic young fighter, like a Greek hero on his way to preordained death, sang his final song.

Ali was the challenger, and he came out first. His entourage moved slowly through the humid African night. The air was thick, the heat close to unbearable. The crowd cheered as Ali made his way to the ring. Black hands reached out and touched him. Ali entered the ring and lifted his gloved fists high above his head.

Foreman and his people jogged to the ring. Foreman was the future of boxing — young, strong, energetic. It looked as if he couldn't get to the ring fast enough. He was the champion from whom Ali had stolen the respect he deserved.

Foreman banged his gloves together in eager anticipation. Ali's vaunted courage seemed more bravado than anything else. A nervous Angelo Dundee pushed on the ropes, checked out the floor, and made sure that all the proper equipment was there in case Ali was hurt.

The obvious strategy was for Ali to move away from Foreman, to hope that after six or seven rounds, if the big man hadn't caught him with one of his thunderous blows, the fight would be at least even. Foreman's fights had always ended within a few rounds; he'd never gone a long distance. Believing that no man could withstand his power, Foreman wanted to simply stand in front of Ali and hit him. Ali hoped to last until the later rounds, when Foreman's power would fade from fatigue and he could prevail with his sharper punches.

"I'm going to run over and punch him in his face," Ali said shortly before the bell rang. "Let him know he's in a fight!"

"No, Champ! No!" Dundee screamed. "You have to dance. Stay away from him."

The bell rang. Ali rushed across the ring and threw a right lead at Foreman. The punch landed, surprising the big man. Ali stood toe-to-toe with Foreman, exchanging blows, beating him to the punch. Foreman's most valuable weapon, his crushing blows, started from way behind his back. Ali wasn't giving him that room. Each time Foreman would bring his fists back, Ali would hit him once, twice, three times. Foreman kept his hands busier, throwing shorter, less effective punches.

The first round was a surprise to Foreman, and to Angelo Dundee, and to the thousands of spectators. Overhand right leads?

"Right leads from a right-handed fighter come from a longer distance," the writer Norman Mailer observed. "When you throw right leads it's telling your opponent that you think you're a lot faster than he is. A lot faster." A right-hand lead from a right-handed fighter has to travel across the body to land on an opponent. A quick left-hand jab, Ali's fastest and best weapon, would have been the logical choice.

Foreman had expected Ali to stay away from him, using all the space he could to keep out of hitting range, and had practiced for weeks "cutting off the ring," moving at angles which would confine Ali to a smaller space. But Ali, in the first round, stood directly in front of Foreman, fighting him man to man, giving him what he thought he wanted. But Ali was beating him to the punch. Foreman was taking more punches than he wanted to, but that suited him just fine. He knew who had the hardest punch. He did. George Foreman, champion.

"You have to dance," Angelo Dundee reminded Ali when he returned to the corner at the end of the first round. "Stay away from him. See what kind of condition he's in. And stay away from the ropes."

The bell for the second round rang. Ali moved quickly to the center of the ring, beat Foreman to the punch with yet another right leader, and then moved away. Foreman followed him to the ropes, fully expecting Ali to slide off and move toward the center of the ring. Instead, Ali leaned against the ropes, throwing light punches in the direction of his opponent. This was what became known as the rope-a-dope. No one had seen this before, a fighter standing still and letting a ferocious puncher unleash the full fury of his blows. Foreman saw Ali cringe and knew he had hurt him. "And then he looked at me," Foreman said, "he had that look in his eyes like he was saying I'm not going to let you hurt me."

Foreman had Ali where he wanted him, against the ropes. He could hear Dundee screaming for his man to move. Foreman set his feet, throwing punches intended to punish Ali's body. He was landing the shorter punches, but every time he tried to unleash the full fury of the longer blows, Ali would again beat him to the punch and make him cover up. Ali was covering up for most of Foreman's punches, letting them hit his arms

Next page: Rumble in the Jungle.

and gloves. He knew other opponents had tried to protect themselves against Foreman's strength, but to no avail.

The next round came with Ali again leaning on the ropes, taking advantage of each time Foreman reached back with his punches by sending a flurry of blows at his taller enemy. Foreman was still punching hard, but not as hard as he had in the gym with his trainer holding the bag. And he was being hit, more than he had ever been hit in his life. Ali's punches were sharp, damaging.

"I realized right then and there he hadn't bought his championship," Foreman later confessed.

The next rounds were repeats of the second, and ringsiders, seeing Foreman swinging away at a nearly stationary Ali, sensed the end was in sight. Ali grabbed Foreman's head and started talking to him.

"Hit harder! Show me something, George!" Ali hissed into Foreman's ear. "That don't hurt! I thought you was supposed to be bad!"

Ali's supporters held their breath as Foreman pounded away.

Then, toward the end of the sixth round, Foreman's blows started to seem less effective. Ali was hitting Foreman harder, and more often. In the eighth round a frustrated Foreman again crowded Ali against the ropes. He threw what he had left. It was not enough. Ali hit the big man hard, and again, and again. The crowd was stunned as Foreman stumbled away, his hands falling down to his sides while Ali clubbed him with overhand rights and sweeping lefts. Foreman pitched forward onto the canvas. The referee picked up the count as Foreman tried to clear his head. Soon the ring was filled with people in wild celebration. The fight was over. Muhammad Ali had knocked out the fierce young champion, George Foreman.

Part IV

A CAREER ENDS

A boxer who experiences a knockout in the first round may be exposed to less cerebral trauma than the boxer that experiences multiple cerebral concussions through-out the duration of a 10-round bout. Boxers most likely to develop punch-drunkenness or chronic neurological in-jury are notorious for being able to take a punch.

— Medical Aspects of Boxing

To everything there is a season, and a time to every pur-pose under the heaven. A time to be born, and a time to die; a time to plant, and a time to pluck up that which is planted.

— Ecclesiastes 3:1-2

THE RING WARRIOR

I n 1974, Muhammad Ali beat Joe Frazier and then, in a stunning upset, defeated the seemingly invincible George Foreman. In March 1975, he fought Chuck Wepner, winning in fifteen rounds. In May of the same year he beat Ron Lyle, and then less than two months later, Joe Bugner. But with the Wepners and the Lyles and the Bugners of the world, the fights were more exhibition than anything else. No one thought these men would have a chance, and the money earned reflected that fact. For Wepner it was a payday and a chance to get publicity for endeavors other than fighting, such as his wholesale beer business. For Lyle it was merely paid entertainment to get beaten up by the most charming, charismatic fighter of all time, and to do it before a Las Vegas crowd with a backdrop of scantily clad showgirls. The only heavyweight who could bring real money, the money derived from television sponsors and filmmakers, was Smokin' Joe Frazier.

Joe Frazier was a warrior, a man whose physical skills and ring knowledge were respected by anyone who knew the game. He always brought his best to a fight, and he brought out the best in Ali. The fight was signed and scheduled to be held just outside of Manila in Quezon City, the Philippines, on September 30, 1975. The event was dubbed the "Thrilla in Manila."

Joe Frazier rose to boxing prominence the hard way. He worked hard and fought hard in Philadelphia gyms before turning professional. He conducted himself as a gentleman at all times and yet, even when he was the champion, even when he had beaten Ali, he never received the acclaim and respect that he felt the championship deserved. Joe Louis had become an American icon. Rocky Marciano, who had never faced a major challenge to his championship, was highly honored and still considered a major figure in American boxing at his death in 1969. Floyd Patterson, too, was highly regarded and warmly received in sports circles. Not only did Joe Frazier feel that he had never received the respect he was due, he believed the problem was one man: Muhammad Ali.

"That old Clay is crazy," Frazier claimed in a 1971 interview for *Sports Illustrated.* "He's something else. He goes around the country, preaching that so-called Black talk. He's a phony. You know what I mean. He calls people ugly. Now what do that have to do with anything?"

Ali had accused Joe Frazier of being an Uncle Tom, a black man who scrapes and bows before whites. It was an unfair charge, and one of Ali's cruelest accusations, meant to take away Frazier's respect among his own people.

Ali also called Joe ugly. Ali called all of his opponents ugly, but with Frazier, he went further. At press conferences, Ali got reporters laughing at Frazier. Before the fight in the Philippines, he carried a little toy gorilla around with him and pulled it out for reporters. He would say that it was Joe Frazier and would hit it while reciting his poems. There had never been a fighter who could talk like Ali. Liston, Patterson, Foreman, and Frazier all fell silent at press conferences while Ali ridiculed them. The only way any of them could shut up the Louisville Lip was to beat him decisively in the ring. Frazier couldn't wait for another chance.

Ali and Frazier — these were warriors. They knew why they were in the Philippines. Ali at thirty-three could see his star in descent. There were few fights left in the legs, and when the legs went, the body would be punished. With each fight he would threaten to quit the game, and after each fight he would be drawn back into the sport he loved. A final fight with Smokin' Joe would be a fitting end.

Frazier had been beaten badly by George Foreman. At thirty-one he had already taken too many beatings, had already spent too much time under medical care. He had little hope of regaining the championship if Foreman held it. Foreman's big punch and youth would impose itself easily on Frazier's style of taking punches in order to give them. *Sportsworld*, the English sports magazine, reported that Frazier's handlers were advising him to retire. What better way out of boxing than a win over Muhammad Ali.

A way out of boxing. Young fighters look for a way in, a way to reap the big rewards that boxing promises. But there comes a time when every fighter needs a way out. To most fighters, that way comes easily. They are never good enough to carry the fighting into that stage at which it becomes truly profitable. They fight a few minor fights, lose, and move on to other jobs. Ironically it is the best of the fighting world who face the most dangers. The questions begin to mount: How many punches are too many? How much wear and tear on the body is too much? When will the body stop healing itself?

"You only have so many fights in you," Archie Moore once said.

A man reaches his physical peak between the ages of seventeen and twenty-eight. During this time he is not only strong, but his body heals quickly. The kidneys recover faster from body punches and resume their task of filtering the blood. The muscles heal and lift the arms to ward off new blows. However, the brain, battered over and over within the skull, does not renew itself, and does not show its damage. When the mind is foggy after a blow it is because the brain is injured. No one knows exactly how much injury a human brain can take before normal human functioning is compromised.

This is no mystery to anyone in the fight game. As Ali himself once observed, "A young fighter doesn't like to look in the face of a scarred, punch-drunk member of the tribe. He might see his own future."

By the time he was thirty-three, Ali had been fighting for over twenty years. Moreover, he had been training all those years, and many in the fight game believed the gym to be more dangerous than the ring.

When would Ali leave boxing?

There were no secrets between Frazier and Ali. Ali knew Frazier would come in relentlessly, throwing bombs from every angle. Frazier knew Ali would move away, and when he couldn't move, would lie on the ropes and hold and grab.

When any fight could be the last, the one to determine the fighter's place in history, the stakes reach almost desperation level. On September 30, 1975, at the Thrilla in Manila, they did.

The beginning of the fight saw Frazier moving in, moving in, pushing Ali back against the ropes. He would take one, two, sometimes four or five punches to the head to get close enough to throw blistering left hooks toward Ali's body. Ali would tie up Frazier as soon as he could, then push away and find another position near the ropes, and let Frazier come in again. This was the rope-a-dope again, but by this time everyone understood what it meant. Ali was willing to lay on the ropes, taking the enormous pain being inflicted on him by Frazier in hopes of being able to retaliate when Joe tired. For the first four rounds Ali looked good, as expected. Then Joe began to get through Ali's defenses. *Whomp! Whomp!* The punches landed on Ali's arms, against the arms he held close to his side.

Whomp! Whomp! A punch to the midsection makes Ali wince. A hook to the side of the head makes him turn his head as he clutches and grabs, trying to get away from Frazier.

Smokin' Joe is confident. He knows he has hurt Ali. He moves in again. The punches from Ali come in bunches. Ali is hurt, but he fights back ferociously. Survival is what counts, but who will survive the punishment? Frazier is still a believer and doesn't think anyone can withstand the blows he is throwing. Ali hits Frazier again and again and again. He wonders how many punches Frazier can take.

For a while it seemed that this time it would be Frazier who would impose his style on Ali. Pound and pound this man, Frazier thought, this Louisville Lip, this stealer of his respect, and he would fall to the canvas, forever beaten.

Ali was in pain, unable to stop the onslaught, his legs

Next page: Thrilla in Manila.

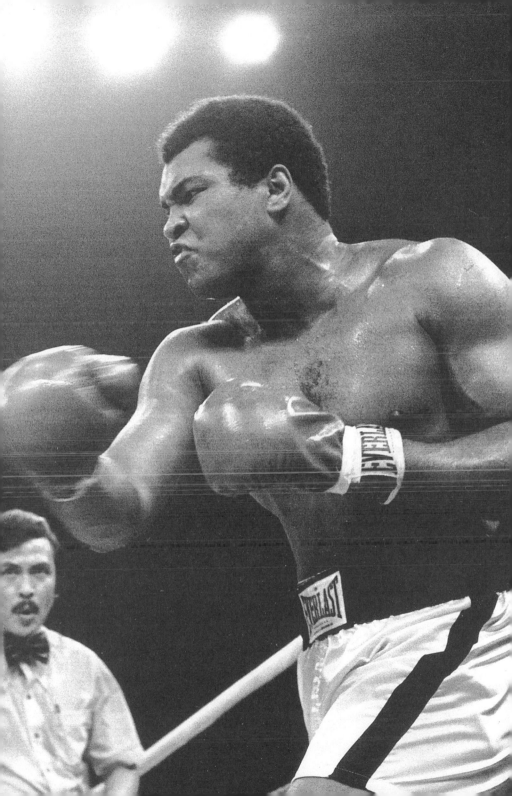

no longer moving as he leaned against the ropes, which he hoped could lend the bounce his legs no longer had. He knew he had to somehow find the strength and courage to battle through the pain and keep his own offense going.

The physical pain was excruciatingly intense. Fans who watch a boxing match often think that fighters don't feel pain the way that "normal" people do. The truth is that professional fighters live with the pain and continue performing at times when most men would be glad to quit and walk away.

What keeps Ali going? The level of oxygen in the air is low and the fighters gasp for breath. Both fighters are hurt and neither wants to quit. Frazier knows that Ali is in agony. Ali, in turn, can see the swelling in Frazier's face and head. He knows that Smokin' Joe is coming into him on little more than courage. Courage that ignites his last bit of strength with body blows that send waves of misery through Ali.

Round twelve. Ali began hitting Frazier with more combinations. Frazier's legs were suddenly as tired as Ali's; his arms were just as heavy. He had thrown his best punches, punches that would have knocked down a wall, and still Muhammad Ali was standing.

Now Ali pushed Frazier's head back with his left hand, measuring the distance between them for the right hand that followed. Frazier staggered once, and again. He wouldn't go down. This was an epic clash of wills, and Frazier would not give in.

The next round saw Frazier slightly disoriented, his eyes puffed up and nearly shut, Ali swinging at will. Smokin' Joe's mouthpiece went flying. Ali moved to the right, toward the closed eye, and sent right hand after right hand into Frazier's badly swollen head. His face was so distended that it looked monstrous under the glaring ring lights.

Frazier's cornerman realized that he couldn't see out of his left eye. His mouthpiece was covered with blood. He was behind on points, and it was obvious that he was too tired to score a knockout. Against his wishes, Joe's corner called the referee over and ended the fight. The contest was scored a technical knockout for Ali.

In Ali's corner there was a sigh of relief.

Sitting on the stool, utterly exhausted, Muhammad Ali had won his most courageous fight. Everything he had, and everything Joe Frazier had, they gave to that fight. "It was the next thing to dying," Ali said later. Neither man would ever be the same again.

After the Thrilla in Manila, Ali and Frazier exchanged expressions of respect and amazement for the other's physical stamina and courage. Ali left the fight with even more respect as a ring warrior than he had previously enjoyed. But people were wondering how much more he could take.

. . . STING LIKE A BEE

The objective of a fighter is to impose his style on his opponent. If he is a "brawler," then he must turn his fights into slugfests in which the ability to punch and take a punch outweighs finesse. In a brawler's career the peak years might well be shortened by the amount of punishment received. The absolute decline of a brawler comes as his major physical skills, the ability to punch and to take a punch, are overcome by younger fighters just reaching their peak.

Ali's style, unique for a heavyweight, was largely dependent on foot and hand movement as he "floated like a butterfly" out of harm's way and moved in quickly to "sting like a bee." The bad form he showed in the ring — leaning away from a punch, keeping his hands too low — was offset by his amazing ability to *move*. This was the style he imposed with relative ease before his forced layoff in 1967. In the twenty-nine fights he won between 1960 and 1967, he had never been hurt. He was twenty-five, at his physical peak, when he was forced out of boxing.

The Ali who returned to the ring in 1970 was twenty-eight, still physically strong, but with a marked difference. His foot speed had slowed considerably during the layoff, as was apparent in his first fight on his return against Jerry Quarry. Against Oscar Bonavena it was a tired Ali who finally stopped the heavyweight from Argentina in the final round.

The fight against twenty-seven-year-old Joe Frazier on March 8, 1971, was a classic match of styles. Frazier kept coming in and, even though he took punches along the way, he was still able to do quite a bit of damage to Ali. Ali could not move quickly or consistently enough to avoid Frazier's blows.

Ali's style began to change. The man who had dominated boxing with his "dancing" speed now began to spend more time flat-footed, using his hand speed to block punches and tie up, or hold opponents who caught him against the ropes until the referee separated them. His 1973 loss to Ken Norton was marked by very little movement on Ali's part, and his win against the plodding muscular ex-marine showed little more.

By 1974, at thirty-two and in the rematch with Joe Frazier, Ali was spending more and more time leaning on the ropes, tying Frazier up when he could, and taking more and more punishment. Ali was using his will — the idea that no matter what punishment he received, he still

would not be defeated — as a substitute for his foot speed. Nowhere was this more evident than in the fight against George Foreman.

Ali's new "style" was based on raw courage, a courage he had shown all his life. As twelve-year-old Cassius Clay in Louisville, he had taken up fighting with Joe Martin, putting himself in harm's way at an early age. He mastered his fear of pain and accepted the discipline needed to become a champion.

His Olympic victory showed Ali exactly what he had. He understood as well as the men wishing to "handle" him that his Olympic gold medal could be turned into a lucrative fighting career if he maintained himself as Cassius Clay and took the route that Joe Louis, Rocky Marciano, Sugar Ray Robinson, and other fighters he admired had taken. He would have been wealthy, respected, and - could have had a predictable career by merely accepting what was being offered to him in exchange for his skills. But Ali lived by his own beliefs. Some sportswriters suggested that he had been "fooled" by the Nation of Islam — that Cassius Clay/Muhammad Ali was being manipulated by people more clever than he was into taking an unpopular stance. But young black men in the 1960s struggled for manhood against often overwhelming odds. In order to maintain the courage of his convictions, Muhammad Ali was willing to take whatever punishment America was willing to hand him.

Ali also had the courage to change the fight game by taking on every fighter on the scene. Few champions had ever done this in the history of fighting. No fighter at any level of the game had the excuse of Ali ducking him to avoid a tough fight.

In the celebration that followed his knockout of George Foreman, the sports media and the world in general exclaimed Ali's genius, though few acknowledged that the rope-a-dope — the technique of resting against the ropes while one's opponent tired himself out swinging — was born more out of necessity than wisdom.

Ali's next three fights after Foreman — against Chuck Wepner, Ron Lyle, and Joe Bugner — saw him extended for longer and longer bouts. At the end of his grueling fourteen-round final fight, the Thrilla in Manila with Joe Frazier in 1975, Ali talked about quitting. But in 1976 Ali fought four more times, two of them fifteen-round fights that took an awful lot out of him. His handlers knew he was being seriously hurt. In 1977, a thirty-five-year-old Muhammad Ali was still fighting. Again, the fights went the full fifteen rounds with Ali winning on decisions.

In 1978, Ali, once more leaning against the ropes and taking far too much punishment from a mediocre but strong fighter, Leon Spinks, lost in fifteen rounds. People watching the fight actually cried to see him being pounded by someone who couldn't have lasted five rounds with The Greatest in his prime. Ali's pride brought him back to the ring with Spinks in September 1978, and he regained his

How many punches are too many? Ali vs. Spinks, September 1978.

world heavyweight crown. This fight, too, was a long fifteen rounds.

Even sportswriters who had not liked Ali during his career now begged him to retire before he was seriously injured. Ali did not fight in 1979, but came back to lose to Larry Holmes on October 2, 1980.

In December 1981, in Nassau, in the Bahamas, an exhausted, beaten Ali lost his last fight. The opponent was Trevor Berbick.

Ali's decline as a fighter was inevitable. The man who loved boxing held on to the sport too long, gave too much credence to the will that had sustained him for so long.

At Ali's final fight, the bout against Berbick, a sportswriter turned to Wali "Blood" Muhammad, Ali's longtime bodyguard, and said, "He's getting hurt, Blood."

"That's right, he is," was the answer.

All America felt the pain.

THE FIGHT OF HIS LIFE

The cameras panned the huge Olympic arena. Floodlights, sweeping wildly across the pulsing crowd, added to the growing excitement. Then a lone figure was spotlighted. He was holding a flaming torch. Muhammad Ali, who had first come to the world's attention at the Olympic games some thirty-six years earlier, lit the Olympic torch. The 1996 Summer Games had begun in Atlanta, Georgia.

A close-up of Muhammad Ali in 1996 showed an impassive face. The sparkle that had illuminated his expression as he mugged for the cameras of *Life* magazine was absent. His hands trembled as he lit the Olympic torch. He then moved slowly, rigidly, away from center stage. Still, the crowd cheered. People were quiet in front of their television sets. Some were moved to tears. Was this the same Muhammad Ali who had stunned the world in 1964 with his knockout of Sonny Liston?

This was the man known for decades as The Greatest. As a young man his star had streaked brilliantly across the skies of America, changing the face of his sport, giving impetus to the dreams of thousands of imitators. Now he seemed as slow as he had once seemed fast, as subdued as he had once been lively. He had once held the heavyweight championship of the world. Now a dread disease held him.

Parkinson's disease is a chronic neurological condition named after Dr. James Parkinson, an English surgeon who first described the illness in 1817. The disease affects certain nerve centers inside the brain, reducing a chemical, dopamine, that is vital to human functioning. The most obvious symptoms of Parkinson's are hands that tremble uncontrollably and a general body stiffness. The sufferer usually moves more slowly than normal, and sometimes the voice is softer. Very often even the face seems frozen in one expression for long periods of time. Well over one million Americans suffer from Parkinson's disease.

Many people feel that Ali's boxing resulted in Parkinson's, but the truth is that no one knows exactly why - people get the disease. The Reverend Billy Graham has Parkinson's, as does Pope John Paul II and the actors Katherine Hepburn and Michael J. Fox, and none of these people were fighters. The disease strikes men and women from all walks of life.

Muhammad Ali at the opening ceremony
of the 1996 Summer Olympics in Atlanta.

Although the disease works very slowly and, to some extent, can be controlled by drugs, there is presently no known cure.

Is it possible that Muhammad Ali's long fight career - could have triggered the disease? The evidence seems to point in that direction, but no one can be sure at this time.

While the cause of Muhammad Ali's condition is questionable, the physical condition of other boxers who fought in the fifties, sixties, and seventies is not. Both Sugar Ray Robinson and Joe Louis, outstanding champions of their day, ended their lives with the severe memory loss and disorientation common to Alzheimer's sufferers. Looking back at other champions, we find that Ezzard Charles, champion after Joe Louis, died from injuries to the spine. Tommy "Hurricane" Jackson, clearly brain damaged at the end of his career, would run through the streets of Queens, New York, training for nonexistent fights against nonexistent opponents. Jerry Quarry, who had fought valiantly against both Muhammad Ali and Joe Frazier, was described as "childlike" when he died at age fifty-three. The number of fighters who end up "punchy," or worse, is the sport's dirty little secret. And it is a secret well-kept by sportswriters and other insiders.

Muhammad Ali has not surrendered to Parkinson's disease. Ali's high profile and his willingness to disclose his condition to the world is one of his bravest, most inspiring acts. In 1997, Ali testified via a written statement before the House Appropriations Subcommittee for the

Department of Labor, Health & Human Services, Education and Related Agencies. The purpose of the hearing was to consider, among other things, whether the federal government should provide $100 million toward research for a cure for Parkinson's disease. The condition is not, given proper care, one that shortens the life of the sufferer, but it is difficult to deal with and often leads to depression as victims find themselves no longer in control of their own bodies. But there is hope that one day the disease will be conquered. If and when that happens, it will probably be because people like Muhammad Ali are fighters. Ali is willing to fight this last, ferocious battle not simply because it will help him, but because it is the right thing to do.

And because doing the right thing is what Muhammad Ali has always been about.

THE LEGACY

What will be the legacy of Muhammad Ali? The man who was named the Greatest Athlete of the 20th Century by *Sports Illustrated* magazine still builds upon his reputation. But legends are made by the people who define them, who look at the lives of people like Muhammad Ali and decide from the vantage point of history whether what they have done is worthwhile. This is why books are written, and why the reader must bring critical judgment to what is written. To understand the considerable contribution of Muhammad Ali, it is necessary to look at him in the context of the times in which he lived.

The boy who was born in Louisville, Kentucky, in 1942, came into a world that few modern young people can understand. The separation of the races under segregation laws that existed in Louisville and in many parts of the United States essentially deemed that in order to survive, black people had to know their "place." The message that this sent to young black boys was that they were somehow inferior human beings. College was a way for some black Americans to claim at least a limited part of the American dream. But for the young men who could not afford college or who did not have the education to attend, life was a constant struggle in which a person had to depend on the good nature of others to survive.

In this sort of hand-me-down existence, the kind of life that young Cassius Clay and his father before him had experienced, the kind of life that Malcolm X had known in Omaha, Nebraska, it is very hard to maintain a sense of pride in either yourself or your people. In this kind of existence, the struggle with self-hatred was often marked by hair straighteners and skin bleaches — tools used to erase racial heritage rather than fight inequality.

Cassius Clay, soon to become Muhammad Ali, had lived life as a second-class citizen. When he won the Olympic gold medal and began receiving the instant attention the medal generated, he realized that, as he put it, he was "kind of special." People who interviewed Ali throughout his long career rarely seemed to recognize that not only did Ali represent, for better or worse, all of black America, but that he *understood* he did. Young black boys and girls across the country wanted to say, like Muhammad Ali, that they were beautiful, that they were pretty. It wasn't vanity that had this handsome young man staring into television cameras and posing for photographers, but rather a desire to broadcast to the world that black was indeed beautiful. In Muhammad Ali, young people found a model for their pride. Ali, in turn, never forgetting where he came from, accepted this role.

At first there were doubters among the black population. When this young man stood up and bragged about how beautiful he was, when he stood up and announced how great he was, would he fail to perform and thereby embarrass all of them? And did the white world understand how easy it was for black people to be embarrassed? Muhammad Ali did. Charles "Sonny" Liston, the ex-crook, was an embarrassment to the NAACP, whose members asked Floyd Patterson not to fight him. They - didn't want Liston to have a chance at the title because they felt that with few redeeming qualities outside of his magnificent punching power, Liston as heavyweight champion would bring shame to the black community.

Muhammad Ali did not embarrass us. He defeated the fierce Sonny Liston when everyone thought he would fall. He followed his heart and joined the Nation of Islam. For some black people Liston's Mob ties were more desirable than Ali's affiliation with the Nation of Islam, which called attention to race at a time when many African Americans, and whites as well, wanted to put race out of the national vocabulary.

Sportswriters wanted Muhammad Ali to play a familiar role. They felt he should be grateful for the chance to compete in the ring, grateful for the chance to make a good living, and grateful for their attention. In short, he was expected to lose his identity as a black person because he was an athlete. Instead, Ali emphasized his position as a black man in boxing and offered himself as an example of what a black man could accomplish.

Muhammad Ali was twenty-two when he won the title in 1964, but he was not the youngest person to win a heavyweight championship — Floyd Patterson had won the championship at twenty-one. But Ali was the most *youthful* heavyweight fighter of all time. Coupled with his incredible media savvy, he appealed to young Americans, white and black. He brought a sincerity to his life and his career that always made him an interesting person to listen to and consider. How could someone who looked that young, who was that attractive, be involved in the most brutal sport known to modern man?

One writer declared in print that the Black Muslims, members of the Nation of Islam, had terrified Ali into not going into the army by suggesting that he would be put into immediate danger of getting killed. This was the kind of nonsense the media concocted to imply that Ali was not capable of making important decisions. However, he clearly made all such decisions, and continues to do so. In the end, Ali's refusal to accept induction into the army was one of the most important statements of the 1960s. He was a celebrity willing to go to jail for his

beliefs. Many young people, white and black, followed his example.

Ali has lived an interesting and exciting life. By no means has he lived a perfect life. His first three marriages ended in divorce. He is the father of seven girls, Hana, Jamillah, Khaliah, Laila, Maryum, Miya, and Rasheeda, and two boys, Muhammad Ali, Jr., and Asaad. While he undoubtedly loved his children, his public life and the constant traveling made a successful family life difficult.

And while he could be vastly entertaining, there have been a number of people he has hurt, especially fellow fighters, by putting them down in public. But he achieved such great popularity that he became a nationally recognized leader of youth — he captivated the minds of American teenagers. He spoke to overflowing crowds on college campuses, yet did not attend college himself. If he had been through the college experience, could he have taken American youth even further in examining the issues of the day?

In his professional life Ali was a standout. Every young fighter who rises above the first amateur rank begins to realize that fighting means the acceptance of pain, and Ali, early on, was willing to do whatever it took to become a champion. He was not, like Sonny Liston or George Foreman, the neighborhood bully skirting the law and beating up smaller kids. Ali was a good kid who knew what he wanted. Through his style, speed, and footwork, he showed the world that intelligence, discipline, and determination could overcome the tactics of sheer power and aggression in heavyweight fighting. And when his speed was not sufficient, he showed in his later fights against Frazier and Foreman that resolve and the courage to accept pain could also be a path to victory.

Perhaps the greatest accomplishment of Muhammad Ali, however, is the one that is impossible to find in the record books. Ali grew as a human being — from the kid in Louisville who needed his bicycle because bus fare wasn't that easy to come by to the young man who successfully dealt with the idea that every word he uttered represented black America — who tried to promote black businesses, pride, and well-being. He gave and still gives much of his time to young people, especially to sick children.

In examining the life of Muhammad Ali, his personal and professional choices, and the fighters he faced in the ring, one wonders if it is morally right to allow young men to risk their health and future for the prizes to be found in a fighting career. So many young people have come to the ring from the farms and from the ghettos — Jews, Italians, blacks, Irish, Latinos — all looking for the elusive dreams of fame and fortune. As the fight game grows, and it is growing, perhaps we don't have the right to deny these young people their chance to succeed. But because we know that in so many cases that quest has ended in the physical ruin of lonely warriors who have dropped off the sports pages and out of the public view, we should at least, as Muhammad Ali has done, try to make sure that when people do sacrifice their bodies, it is not their only way to secure human dignity.

Courage does not mean letting go of fear. It means having the will to face one's fears, to face the dangers in one's life, and to venture forward to do that which is morally right. Writers have said that Ali was afraid of Liston, that he was afraid of going into the army, that he was afraid of turning away from the Nation of Islam. There were things of which he was afraid, but he was big enough, courageous enough, to face everything that came his way. He has been knocked down in his life, and he has had the courage to rise.

Ali died on June 3, 2016, at the age of 74. He remained a deeply religious man until his death. As a Muslim, he prayed five times a day and talked about his religion to anyone who was interested. He lived with Parkinson's disease, which impaired his speech and movement, for more than thirty years, and was a supporter of the National Parkinson's Foundation, lending his name and time to yet another big fight.

Whatever he did, Ali was always a man of outstanding character. He always did what he believed to be the right thing. It is the most that anyone can ask of a life.

Everything I do has a purpose, all of God's beings have a purpose. Others may know pleasure, but pleasure is not happiness. It has no more importance than a shadow following a man.

— **Muhammad Ali, 1942–2016**

PHOTO CREDITS

BIBLIOGRAPHY

Ali, Muhammad and Richard Durham. The Greatest: My Own Story. New York: Random House, 1975.

Arai, Tim, Joseph Peters, and Stanley Wilde, eds. Muhammad Ali: In His Own Words. New York: Pinnacle books, 1975.

Bingham, Howard. Muhammad Ali, A Thirty Year Journey. New York: Simon & Schuster, 1993.

Cantu, Robert C., ed. Boxing and Medicine. Champaign, IL: Human Kinetics, 1995.

Hauser, Thomas. Muhammad Ali: His Life and Times. New York: Simon & Schuster, 1991.

Jordan, Barry D., ed. Medical Aspects of Boxing. Boca Raton, FL: CRC Press, 1993.

Miller, John and Aaron Kenedi. Muhammad Ali, Ringside. Boston: Little Brown, 1999.

Pacheco, Ferdie. Muhammad Ali: A View From the Corner. New York: Birch Lane Press, 1992.

Reemtsma, Jan Philipp. More Than a Champion: The Style of Muhammad Ali. New York: Vintage, 1998.

Remnick, David. King of the World: Muhammad Ali and the Rise of the American Hero. New York: Vintage, 1998.

Roberts, James and Alexander Skutt. The Boxing Register: International Boxing Hall of Fame Official Record Book. Ithaca, NY: McBooks Press, 1999.

Tanner, Michael. Ali in Britain. Edinburgh: Mainstream Publishing, 1995.

THE FIGHT CHRONOLOGY

DATE	LOCATION	OPPONENT	RESULT/ ROUNDS	
1960				
Oct 29	Louisville	Tunney Hunsaker	W	6
Dec 27	Miami Beach	Herb Siler	KO	4
1961				
Jan 17	Miami Beach	Tony Esperti	TKO	3
Feb 7	Miami Beach	Jim Robinson	TKO	1
Feb 21	Miami Beach	Donnie Fleeman	TKO	7
Apr 19	Louisville	Lamar Clark	KO	2
Jun 26	Las Vegas	Duke Sabwedong	W	10
Jul 22	Louisville	Alonzo Johnson	W	10
Oct 7	Louisville	Alex Mitcff	TKO	6
Nov 29	Louisville	Willi Besmanoff	TKO	7
1962				
Feb 10	New York	Sonny Banks	TKO	4
Feb 28	Miami Beach	Jack Wagner	TKO	4
Apr 23	Los Angeles	George Logan	TKO	4
May 19	New York	Billy Daniels	TKO	7
Jul 20	Los Angeles	Alejandro Lavorante	KO	5
Nov 15	Los Angeles	Archie Moore	TKO	4
1963				
Jan 24	Pittsburgh	Charlie Powell	KO	3
Mar 13	New York	Doug Jones	W	10
Jun 18	London, England	Henry Cooper	TKO	5
1964				
Feb 25	Miami Beach	Sonny Liston	TKO	7
	(Won World Heavyweight Title)			

1965

May 25	Lewiston, ME	Sonny Liston	KO	1
	(Retained World Heavyweight Title)			
Nov 22	Las Vegas	Floyd Patterson	TKO	12
	(Retained World Heavyweight Title)			

1966

Mar 29	Toronto, Canada	George Chuvalo	W	15
	(Retained World Heavyweight Title)			
May 21	London, England	Henry Cooper	TKO	6
	(Retained World Heavyweight Title)			
Aug 6	London, England	Brian London	TKO	3
	(Retained World Heavyweight Title)			
Sept 10	Frankfurt, German	Karl Mildenberger	TKO	12
	(Retained World Heavyweight Title)			
Nov 14	Houston	Cleveland Williams	TKO	3
	(Retained World Heavyweight Title)			

1967

Feb 6	New York	Ernie Terrell	W	15
	(Retained World Heavyweight Title)			
Mar 22	New York	Zora Folley	TKO	7
	(Retained World Heavyweight Title)			

1968–1969

(inactive)

1970

Oct 26	Atlanta	Jerry Quarry	TKO	3
Dec 7	New York	Oscar Bonavena	TKO	15

1971

Mar 8	New York	Joe Frazier	L	15
	(Lost World Heavyweight Title)			
Jul 26	Houston	Jimmy Ellis	TKO	12
	(Won Vacant NABF Heavyweight Title)			
Nov 17	Houston	Buster Mathis	W	12
	(Retained NABF Heavyweight Title)			

Dec 26	Zurich, Switzerland	Jurgen Blin	KO	7
1972				
Apr 1	Tokyo, Japan	Mac Foster	W	15
May 1	Vancouver, BC	George Chuvalo	W	12
	(Retained NABF Heavyweight Title)			
Jun 27	Las Vegas	Jerry Quarry	TKO	7
	(Retained NABF Heavyweight Title)			
Jul 19	Dublin, Ireland	Al "Blue" Lewis	TKO	11
Sept 20	New York	Floyd Patterson	TKO	7
	(Retained NABF Heavyweight Title)			
Nov 21	Stateline, NV	Bob Foster	KO	8
	(Retained NABF Heavyweight Title)			
1973				
Feb 14	Las Vegas	Joe Bugner	W	12
Mar 31	San Diego	Ken Norton	L	12
	(Lost NABF Heavyweight Title)			
Sept 10	Los Angeles	Ken Norton	W	12
	(Retained NABF Heavyweight Title)			
Oct 20	Jakarta, Indonesa	Rudy Lubbers	W	12
1974				
Jan 28	New York	Joe Frazier	W	12
	(Retained NABF Heavyweight Title)			
Oct 30	Kinshasa, Zaire	George Foreman	KO	8
	(Retained World Heavyweight Title)			
1975				
Mar 24	Cleveland	Chuck Wepner	TKO	15
	(Retained World Heavyweight Title)			
May 16	Las Vegas	Ron Lyle	TKO	11
	(Retained World Heavyweight Title)			
Jul 1	Kuala Lampur, Malaysia	Joe Bugner	W	15
	(Retained World Heavyweight Title)			
Oct 1	Quezon, Philippines	Joe Frazier	TKO	14

(Retained World Heavyweight Title)

1976

Feb 20	San Juan, Puerto Rico	Jean Coopman	KO	5

(Retained World Heavyweight Title)

Apr 30	Landover, MD	Jimmy Young	W	15

(Retained World Heavyweight Title)

May 24	Munich, Germany	Richard Dunn	TKO	5

(Retained World Heavyweight Title)

Sept 28	New York	Ken Norton	W	15

(Retained World Heavyweight Title)

1977

May 16	Landover, MD	Alfredo Evangelista	W	15
Sept 29	New York	Ernie Shavers	W	15

1978

Feb 15	Las Vegas	Leon Spinks	L	15

(Lost World Heavyweight Title)

Sept 15	New Orleans	Leon Spinks	W	15

(Regained World Heavyweight Title)

1980

Oct 2	Las Vegas	Larry Holmes	TKO'd	11

(For Vacant World Heavyweight Title)

1981

Dec 11	Nassau, Bahamas	Trevor Berbick	L	10

Source: Roberts, James and Alexander Skutt. *The Boxing Register: International Boxing Hall of Fame Official Record Book.* Ithaca, NY: McBooks Press, 1999.

INDEX